If the Delta Was the Sea

Other Books by Dick Lourie

Ghost Radio [with companion CD, *Ghost Radio Blues*] (Hanging Loose)

Anima (Hanging Loose)

4-Telling [with Robert Hershon, Emmett Jarrett, and Marge Piercy] (The Crossing Press)

Letter to Answer (Unicorn)

Lies (Radical America)

Stumbling (The Crossing Press)

The Dream Telephone (The Crossing Press)

If the Delta Was the Sea

Dick Lourie

Hanging Loose Press
Brooklyn, New York

Published by Hanging Loose Press, 231 Wyckoff Street, Brooklyn, New York 11217-2208. All rights reserved. No part of this book may be reproduced without the publisher's written permission, except for brief quotations in reviews.

www.hangingloosepress.com

Printed in the United States of America
10 9 8 7 6 5 4 3 2 1

Hanging Loose Press thanks the Literature Program of New York State Council on the Arts for a grant in support of the publication of this book.

Cover art by Robin Tewes
Cover design by Marie Carter

Acknowledgments
Some of these poems have appeared in *The Arkansas Review, Hanging Loose, The Journal of Popular Music Studies, Lungfull!,* and *Valley Voices.*

Library of Congress Cataloging-in-Publication Data

Lourie, Dick
  If the Delta was the sea / Dick Lourie.
    p. cm.
  ISBN 978-1-934909-02-7 -- ISBN 978-1-934909-01-0 (pbk.)
  1. Delta (Miss. : Region)--Poetry. I. Title.
PS3562.O83138 2009
811'.54--dc22
                              2008046583

Sixty percent of all author's royalties from this book will be donated to organizations and groups in Clarksdale, Mississippi.

Produced at The Print Center, Inc. 225 Varick St., New York, NY 10014, a non-profit facility for literary and arts-related publications. (212) 206-8465

for Abby

and for
Big Jack Johnson, who brought me to Clarksdale
John Ruskey, who opened the doors
Robert Birdsong, who took me inside

If the Delta Was the Sea: Introduction

This book is the record of an extended encounter between the Mississippi Delta, particularly the city of Clarksdale, and one poet/ blues sax player, myself. I'm not a native, but in 1997, when I first went there to play in Clarksdale's annual Sunflower Blues festival, I was generously welcomed into the local blues community. I soon became interested in many other aspects of Delta history and culture besides the music; and since my first visit I've been spending several weeks there every year. My poems, written over the past decade, reflect the breadth of my experience and the richness of the area.

* * *

Growing up in the Northeast, I had little knowledge of the Delta. When I got there, I soon realized that my ideas about the area, based on what I had read and heard, ranged from simplistic to just wrong.

Certainly the grinding poverty I had read about still exists (alongside a sharply contrasting affluence). It's no secret that this area is among the poorest in the country: One of the last times Clarksdale received national notice was as a featured stop—perhaps not the most appropriate term—on President Clinton's famous "Poverty Tour" of America. And the landscape offers plenty of the trademark swamps, shacks, dirt roads, and cotton fields that so frequently appear in picturesque renderings of the Delta. I was not, however, prepared for what else I found: green lawns, deep quiet lakes, gorgeous night skies, universities, art galleries, and thriving (some more than others, to be sure) small cities.

As for the music, I was familiar with articles like the one in the *New York Times* headlined "Blues Is Dying in the Place It Was Born." But what I found when I arrived was not only that the blues is alive and well, but also that some of its practitioners are young teenagers carrying on the tradition.

I had also imagined the Delta as sharply divided between a distinct pair of local cultures, white and black, each isolated from the other, and both struggling to cope with the stubbornly persistent legacy of racism. What I discovered was not that simple. Yes, the consciousness of race and of history is always present, but cultural elements cannot simply be separated into "white" or "black." I was surprised to find that, for more than a hundred years, a variety of ethnic groups has created a lively mix of cultures throughout the Delta.

Finally, I was embarrassed to learn that even my sense of geography was wrong: the Mississippi Delta (more accurately the Yazoo-Mississippi Delta) that I was headed for on my first trip is not at the mouth of the river, but instead is a flood plain in northwest Mississippi. The nearest big city is not New Orleans, but Memphis—which, when you think about it, explains a lot.

* * *

Although I would certainly be gratified if my poems were to help correct such misconceptions—and while Delta facts, Delta history, and Delta people do appear here in profusion—the book's main focus is on my own experience there as a poet and musician. I observed the life of the city, I played with local musicians, I read the daily newspaper, and I researched materials about the culture and history of the Delta.

And whether a particular poem springs from a long night at a blues club or a long coffee shop breakfast with friends the next day, I have tried to be there as a participant, not simply a witness. Throughout this last ten or so years, I have had, of course, many conversations with friends and acquaintances: A number of the poems in the book include transcriptions of these talks, thus incorporating pieces of oral history. Sometimes I think of my time in the Delta as one long, continuous conversation.

In seeking to explore Clarksdale and the Delta as deeply and widely as an outsider can hope to, one of my goals—a familiar one for poets—has been to find the universal within the particular. In other words, I hope that this book about one small area of the planet will have a deeper and wider resonance. And I hope that the poems will in some measure repay the generosity shown me by the many people I have met there, and that the book will contribute to an appreciation of the richness of the Delta's history and culture.

Fragments

On the Way to Clarksdale, Questioned by Airport Security
Q: "What's that, a rocket launcher?"
A: "It's a tenor sax but, used correctly, it can be a rocket launcher."

Inside Joke
First Musician: "What time is the gig tonight?"
Second Musician: "Don't ask me that."
Third Musician: "Remember, you're in Clarksdale now."

Email Reminder from B.L.
"Did you know that the Delta was in fact once covered by the sea?"

Big Jack Johnson Improvises
It's 60 degrees in Clarksdale but snowing in Boston
Boys, it's snowing in Boston, I'm just sitting here wondering
How's my friend Dick going to get home

Nostalgia Works in Mysterious Ways
Ashley: "Yes, we've traveled a long road, haven't we, Scarlett? Oh,
the lazy days—the warm still country twilight, the high soft Negro
laughter from the quarters. The golden warmth and security of
those days."
　　　　　—Gone with the Wind (the movie)

And So Does Irony
"The engineer was the only white man in the South who did not
know all there was to know about Negroes."
　　　　　—Walker Percy, *The Last Gentleman*

Inscribed on a Plaque at the Corner of Riverside and West Second Street
Spirit on high, come down, come down
And rest Thy Hand upon this town
And let Thy Love flow full and free
Through human vessels just like me.
　　　　　—Louise Moss Montgomery, resident of Clarksdale,
　　　　　　　and Mississippi poet laureate, 1973-78

Contents

Transformations

When He Wakes

L'Envoi

Meetings at the Crossroads

If the Delta Was the Sea

> *Yes! Thank God; human feeling is like the mighty*
> *rivers that bless the earth; it does not wait for*
> *beauty—it flows with resistless force, and brings*
> *beauty with it.*
> —George Eliot, *Adam Bede*

"if the river was whiskey" Big T sings
one night at Red's juke joint "and I was a
diving duck"   a good old favorite from
both black and white country traditions   "I'd
dive to the bottom and never come up"
I'm standing next to T playing the sax
and—blues being my meditative state—
I think to myself: extraordinary

metaphor!   to be conditional and
transformative at the same time   and as
usual when at Red's I also feel
immersed in Clarksdale   so my mind shifts and
spins the image till it comes to rest on
the mysteries around me: if the river
was Clarksdale what would I be?   (stranger from
such a different place poking around

outsider trying to peer inside)   would I
be Twain on the Mississippi   godlike
pilot   sure hand   every rock and shoal
clear in his mind?   or Rimbaud's drunken boat
floating unguided toward those phantasmic
ocean visions?   and knowing that each choice
bears its own gifts   and dangers   should I dive
or sink   or drift?   and if the river was

Clarksdale the Delta would be the sea   (as indeed
it once was)   vast and   in many stories primal
 "darkness upon the face of the deep" while the
earth is still "without form"   and if the Delta
was the sea then Clarksdale   every town   roads
houses   forests   fields   even Red's   all would
be mingled with it   as waters of the
Mississippi flow to the Gulf   and we

looking out over the Delta Sea from
our narrow lives would think it endless
and always changeable: in the era
when cotton is king it's a gleaming sea
white in the sun   or sometimes we look beneath:
layers   waves of black and brown topsoil   rich
deepest in the world we're told   calm and smooth
or on some days the surface rough with old

Indian mounds or anonymous clumps
of earth where slaves are buried   and other
days maybe close to twilight the Delta
Sea is golden   trick of the light or a
reflection of great wealth   and in the depths
beyond our vision the registry of
bones: the dead   those newly wept for and down
ever deeper   thousands of years back to

the Bronze Age—famously democratic
this undersea city of bones unhinged
from age   race   history   cause of death   and
by now the "sea-change into something rich and
strange" has as promised transfigured them all
to coral and pearl   and as my meditations
come to rest back where I started at Red's
listening to T—if the river was

Clarksdale and the Delta was the sea then
tonight it would all be intense blue   deep
blue Delta Sea   eternal   the purest though
darkest blue of blues   I might never come up

16

Geography Lesson on First Visit to Clarksdale, Mississippi

"The Mississippi Delta begins in the lobby of the Peabody Hotel in Memphis and ends on Catfish Row in Vicksburg."
—David Cohn, *Where I Was Born and Raised*

I'd always pictured the Mississippi
Delta just at the river's mouth—never
too clear on geography that's all I
remembered about deltas from sixth grade
but on my first trip the plane lands far north
of the Gulf   in Memphis: this Delta turns out
to be a northwest Mississippi flood plain
across from Arkansas and almost in

Tennessee but I'm still vague on precise
geography so it's lucky the map
in my rented car says once out of south
Memphis just go straight down Route 61

I guess I should have figured it all out
before—"Blues Boy" King chose Memphis over
New Orleans   and what Elvis Presley in-
haled along Beale Street was Delta fragrance

which is to say more ribs than magnolia
more guitar than piano   or is that
just in my own mind: first impressions do
leave the deepest marks and in Clarksdale mine
is the Delta Blues Museum workshop
where Doctor Mike James is teaching blues to

12-year-old musicians: seeing my sax
case Mike just waves me to come and join them

at this point I have found the Delta and
what's more I know exactly where I am

Rights

"Father...we have been a happy people
under your care and protection until
of late the State of Mississippi has
extended her laws over us and we

are threatened...altho we love our white Brothern
we cannot see in the extention of
these state laws over us anything but
injustice and oppression"   after the

Chickasaw wrote this to Andrew Jackson
in 1831 they were moved west—
in Mississippi the white pioneers
thrived with black slaves   cleared swamps   planted cotton

after the war for ten years or so the
slaves—now freedmen—owned land   voted under
federal protection until the deal that
gave some rights back to Mississippi and

then as foreseen by the Chickasaw she
extended her laws over them   wings of
the great white bird   reawakened power
of the state   beak and claw   the hooded eyes

In 1883 Mark Twain Observes Sharecropping But Misses Some Crucial Details

almost twenty years beyond slavery
Mark Twain—that shrewd inhabitant of two
centuries—looks at the future of the
Delta in *Life on the Mississippi*

though blacks now receive cash for their labors
it just ends up   he says   in the hands of
Jewish merchants keen to sell them things they
don't need and at inflated prices too

so they've worked hard but they're still poor and soon—
destitute and discouraged—they pack up
their families   hail the next riverboat
and move on to another plantation

thus the planter loses experienced
hands   the blacks remain poor   and only the
"Israelites" as Twain calls them get rich
but   he says   a better day is hoped for:

some New England investors plan to buy
10,000 fertile acres   treat field
hands well   and establish stores right on their
plantation to sell goods at fair prices

which   benefiting both planters and blacks
will be good for everyone but the Jews:
did that old debunker Twain really—like
all those others—fall for "the Jews did it"?

you could laugh if you had a strong sense of
irony and lacked all human feeling:
it does seem like a nasty joke has been played
on someone and I know it's not Mark Twain

Development at the Crossroads

for Sherman

*Note: In a well-known blues legend with both
European and African roots, a musician seeks out an
infernal midnight bargain at a crossroads somewhere
in the Delta. The Devil makes him the best blues
guitar player in the world—but only in exchange for
his eternal soul. The story became attached to
Robert Johnson sometime after his death.*

*"The Gentleman held the majority of stock in
Robert Johnson's soul and had chased Robert
Johnson for decades. Since 1938, the year he faked
his death by poisoning and made his escape, Johnson
had been running from the Gentleman, who
narrowly missed him at every stop."*
—Sherman Alexie, *Reservation Blues*

of course no one knows at exactly which
intersection Robert Johnson is said
to have taken the most costly guitar
lesson in the history of the blues
but legend says that the exchange occurred
somewhere near here   so Clarksdale has staked its
own modest claim right where 61 meets
49   and this attracts visitors

which is important since Clarksdale's poor—few
casinos to boost the tax base like elsewhere
in the Delta (speaking of deals with—but
that's another story) so it's no shock
to hear prominent local businessmen
speak of upscaling the crossroads   which is

marked now only by a signpost bearing
as coat of arms two blue guitars crossing

one entrepreneur was heard to say that
there's nothing at this dusty spot but "a
gas station and a doughnut shop"   an in-
cautious remark   I see Robert Johnson
road-weary   years of dodging the Hellhound
on his trail   he's come home to the crossroads
it's 4 a.m.   he looks around slowly
"hmm   nothing here but a gas station and

a doughnut shop—but that fragrance—more like
Heaven than Hell"   Delta Donut has just
opened for the day   Robert Johnson steps
in   gently lays down his guitar   weeps for joy

the kind counter woman helps him choose a
dozen for his travels: the delicate
glaze   lemon-filled   éclair   apple fritter
and of course devil's food   she knows he's poor
and desperate   for him the coffee's free:
he smiles   slings the guitar across his back
takes the white box in one hard hand   hot cup
in the other   walks down the road   and looks

back   it's dawn: then—his voice like the knife's edge—
"a curse falls" Robert Johnson says "on those
who mess with this place   blessed by me Delta
Donut abides here beneath my outstretched wings"

Intersections

for Steve Seidel

as gatekeeper between the spirit world
and ours Legba frequents crossroads and could
have been the creator of Delta blues
since the first one we know   the refrain Mr.
Handy overheard   is "I'm goin' where
the Southern cross the Dog" and if   as we're
told   it was Legba (though miscast as the
devil) who taught Robert Johnson the blues

in return for his young black soul right here
in Clarksdale Mississippi—that explains
the power of this place where 61
Highway crosses 49 and where all
we have to offer is our old white souls
which we're not yet ready to trade in   still
we seem drawn to this crossroads in Clarksdale—
where children now are taught to play the blues

not in exchange for the soul but to shore
it up: so that generosity can
live next door to racism and survive
the strain   and poverty can be leavened
sometimes with drums and guitars—so let us
rest again here at this intersection
and reflect on the blues: and if Legba
comes to us at midnight we'll decide then
what it is that we want to ask him for

Notes from the Future: Taken from the Journals of Imaginary Researchers Exploring Ancient Clarksdale, Mississippi

Journal I: Prehistory–Circa AD 1870

stone spear points many thousands of years old:
these are hunters of bison and mammoth—
later   though still nomadic   life gets more
complex: they make beads   tools to crack nuts

then real settlements   ceramics   houses
with hearths   concentric tiers of earth ridges
around a central plaza   while objects
of Gulf Coast conch   Great Lakes copper lodged in

burial mounds suggest trade with other
regions   and after a while: centralized
government   clear traces of squash   beans   corn
planted by people whose names we still know

Note: By now, however, these names have been almost forgotten. Biloxi, Chickasaw, Choctaw, Coroas, Creek, Grigras, Natchez, Ofo, Pascagoula, Quapaw, Tioux, Tunica—They are all called "Indians" by the Europeans who come sweeping through the continent to assert their dominance. In this Delta, that dominance takes the form of a system dependent on slaves brought from Africa, and on the exile of most of the surviving "Indians" to less fertile areas. Now swamps are drained, more land is cleared for planting, and the first signs of town life appear. Settlers prosper among the vast cotton fields worked by the slaves and the plantation homes paid for by the cotton. Everything about this way of life fades or is transformed after the destruction of slavery by war.

Journal II: Circa AD 1870–AD 2100

Note: Early archaeologists and historical records have established that on this site, from the Stone Age until at least the year AD 2100, there developed a remarkable confluence of cultures which has been called—after its major city—the "Clarksdale Civilization." Unfortunately, the latest and highest stage of its development, through the 20th and 21st centuries and perhaps even beyond, is not well-documented. Consequently, our team of scientists was asked to excavate here for whatever might help us learn more.

what we've dug up: splinters of railroad track
bricks from commercial buildings   an oil mill
saloon brass   scraps of mail in several
languages   suggesting more immigrants

so it's a thriving town right into the
1900s in spite of war   fire   flood
maps refer to it as the "county seat"
major roads crossed here—now faint ghostly paths

and the cotton still had to be worked: some
altered kind of servitude maybe   since
remnants of shacks from this period
look very much like the old slave quarters

* * *

Note: Still later, some of these crude cabins have apparently been moved from their original locations in or near the cotton fields, and their function has changed. To our surprise, they seem to have been repaired, rebuilt, and adapted—with electricity, air conditioning, new furniture, indoor plumbing—for use as hotel suites, during what we call the "Tourist Period."

and even after machines (iron shards
in the dirt under our feet) have replaced
most field labor   that stubborn culture persists
right alongside the more dominant one:

apart   says our anthropologist   but
not isolated from it—often in
old framed family pictures we still see
one group caring for the other's children—

and though residential patterns show clear
lines of division   the two cultures in
fact by this time are so tightly inter-
woven as to be inseparable

* * *

*Note: It's not known how deep each culture penetrates the other, or
whether they even realize it, or if such fusion, born from the heat
of their convergence, is found elsewhere; but here in 20th-century
Clarksdale the entwining of African and European roots is undeniable.
We infer this from our most precious contemporary source: the frail
crumbling day-to-day newspapers our archivist is carefully restoring.
It is a slow process, but already we've learned a good deal.*

these newspapers for instance show that the
frequent rituals celebrating each
culture's characteristic music share
a crazed attachment to the guitar (hence

the snarl of rusted steel strings we dug up)
and we've learned that "whites" and "blacks"   as they call
themselves   cooperate in governing
the city—a striking change from its past

and that in each of the two religious
systems some elements of both Europe
and Africa coexist   (thus in all
the churches a similar god presides)

and that the most revered of staple foods—
worshipped   debated   contested with the
fervor of Greek Olympic Games   consumed
like water—is common to both cultures

* * *

Note: A recent discovery confirms that this last observation about the significance and status of "ribs" has not been exaggerated: Artifacts and census records make it evident that, as noted above, many parts of the city are predominantly occupied by one "race" or the other. Nevertheless, no matter where we dig, we always find, everywhere, these well-chewed animal bones—along with traces of what appears to be some kind of powerful ceremonial sauce.

on the other hand separation is
sometimes mandated—the word "Only" scrawled
on fragments of signs in public places—
and though laws change   their effects may linger

and still   near the end of the century
bitterness persists in letters to the
newspaper arguing over what is
or is not represented by a flag

* * *

now that the excavations are done we're
waiting for our archivist to finish
restoring newspapers as far as the end
of the 21st century to know

more about Clarksdale at this period
and the precarious balance between
the blending and the pulling apart of
its two cultures   and more personally:

over the life of this project many
of our team members have come to feel an
attachment for the whole city and all
of its people   so here at the site we

wait more anxiously than we had foreseen
discussing all the possibilities

speculating   hoping that this ancient
civilization did continue to

thrive: and the good news this morning is from
our analytical chemists (who've been
fascinated with the rib bone samples)—
they're now close to identifying all

the components of that sauce   which means that
we can hope to at least imagine the
intensity of that Clarksdale fusion
at its height   since all of us now believe

that above everything it was these shared
tastes which formed the most crucial confluence:
as intimate   profound   and familiar
as lovers eating from each other's plate

The Camel Chronicles

An Improbable Website Involves Me In More of Clarksdale's Mysteries, Its Connection with the World, and An Immense Debtorship

Prologue

"Heated discussion broke out on Tuesday
morning at the Khan on Highway 61
(commonly known as Chamoun's Rest Haven)
between several camel herders and
plow jockeys over recent news of a
camel trade in Muscat, Oman"   thus begins
the fable on this website that Robert
thought would amuse me: fourteen humorous

episodes called *The Camel Chronicles*
linked to Clarksdale's official home page and
claiming to be news from the (non-existent)
Clarksdale Online Register   the story
(reported anonymously) takes place
in 1996–97—though
it's 2002 before I see it:
these particular *Chronicles* are set

in this local restaurant   the kind where
the same people can be counted on to
show up at the same time every day: a
de facto social club with its own codes

habits   customs   inside jokes   and Robert
assures me that all the characters in the *Camel*
Chronicles are real people   though exaggerated—
like politicians in the ancient Greek

comedies   and in the same way these purportedly
true accounts begin with fact   slip into
fiction   end up leaving us with some taste
of truth   sweet and bitter at the same time
and these tales   still here years after they were
created—wherever "here" is on the
Internet—resemble history too:
a thing done   or its effects   can remain

long afterward and (as George Meredith
observed) things done have a way of incurring
"immense debtorship"   as do things set down
spoken   or even just suggested   so
these *Chronicles*   having incurred their debt
hold it before us like that tree in the woods
always in the act of falling   always
noiseless until someone listens—and to

witness   read   or reflect on a thing done
is to take on some of its debtorship
as if you were finally hearing the
tree fall   so in this light satire I hear
Clarksdale speaking about itself   Clarksdale
which (like the world) boasts its own record of
discord   sweat   glory   shame   justice   laughter
wealth   unspeakable acts   poverty   hope

and I incur some of its debt   weaving
my way through these jokes   these tall tales that are
nevertheless showing us in their way
something about the world and what is owed

Act I: At the Rest Haven: Honor Is Defended and Battle Is Joined

the dispute at the restaurant breaks out
when some in the breakfast crowd take offense
at this reported extravagance: close
to four hundred thousand dollars paid for
a "racing camel"   restaurant owner
Chafik Chamoun uses the occasion
to bring up what is evidently a
recurring   perhaps classic argument

"Which you think is faster: camel or horse?"
"Any good...Southern American" says
Bobby Huggins "knows a horse is faster"
and even in Arabia   says Buck Falls
"they ride horses for speed...Camels...carry
the baggage"   the narrator calls Bobby
Huggins a "lettuce dealer" and Buck Falls
a "feudal landlord"   part of the fun here

are these epithets—which mean nothing to
me of course since I don't know these people—
but I keep on reading through the "in" jokes
and arcane allusions   maybe it's just
the poet's voyeurism: a kind of
eavesdropping   the way I like to nurse my
coffee while at the next table there's talk
of rainstorms   divorce   fish   jobs lost   floor wax

nothing of interest and everything
of interest because I'm not supposed
to hear it   and because from a distance
how else could I learn about these strangers?

tension builds: Chafik drags on his Turkish
cigarette "I dunn know" he says as if
(the author notes) wishing to keep the
argument open   and someone just called

"the Preacher" looks up from his "sacred scrolls":
"the horse is faster...the Bible tells me
so"   "Red! What you t'ink?" Chafik appeals to
Red Bradham   who observes that camels have

longer legs—the Preacher on his way out
(in response to "a distant bell") gets the
last word "what does an auto parts dealer"
he snaps "know about camels and horses?"

* * *

this episode—as a demonstration
of its own veracity—includes links
to the article on racing camels
that first gave offense and to the website
of the Rest Haven itself which offers
a detailed daily schedule starting at
5:30 a.m. with "camel herders
plowmen and a preacher" going on to

"peddlers poachers and poorboy gamblers" then
"village elders (and a few idiots)"—
these groups respectively at 7 and
9—followed by the 10 o'clock crowd of
"amateur politicians & general
liars" "caravan feeding" (noon) then the
3 p.m. "tall tale story hour" and "last
call for java and baklava" at 5

so with all this kind of desert-movie
imagery the restaurant is in
on the joke too   evidently   as if
laying claim to a share of the fable—
there's also a brief bio of Chafik
and his wife Louise in the context of
the Lebanese community that's been
part of Mississippi for many years

certainly this is more than some twisted
testament to multiculturalism
in the Delta—though I think that's here too
as well as just joking with friends   but beyond
the casual and the comic   under
the Delta pride is Clarksdale wishing to
lay claim to its connection with the world
which of course always ends up as the

proverbial mixed blessing   and this is
part of what I mean by "immense debtorship":
in 1996 you could fool around
with good-natured humor about Arabs
and camels and caravans but of course
now when that tree falls it echoes with grief
terror   death   war   torture   life under threat—
so one would not care to make such jokes   but

this brings us back to George Meredith whose
exact words were "Sentimentalists are they who
seek to enjoy Reality without incurring
the Immense Debtorship for a thing done"
thus—as a non-sentimentalist—I'm
stuck with the Internet illusion of
an eternal present   where these jokes
exist along with all the other stuff that's

real about Clarksdale—revelatory
in fact if one only pays attention—
as for whether or not you will decide to
take on a share of the debt   to reject
or welcome sentimentalism   all
I can do here is bring you close up to
where the tree is falling   I can't know
if you'll choose to hear anything at all

❉

Thoroughly Mixed

Thinking About Clarksdale

outside Clarksdale in a vast cotton field—
the dirt road damp   my shoes would stay muddy
for weeks—we saw the unmarked slave burial
ground   its hump of scrub adrift in that white sea

doing the mental arithmetic I
calculated it might actually be
possible to meet in Clarksdale the last
grandchild of a slave buried in this place

and I thought this over—it means of course
that a grandchild of the planter who owned
this slave could still also be around   these
two old people might live just blocks apart

then I thought how—as we used to say—I
can't get my head around Clarksdale   that is:
the idea of these two people maybe
eating at the same restaurant is strange

then I thought well on the other hand their
grandparents could have had sex together
so these two might really be half-cousins
but that made Clarksdale seem even harder

to grasp   then—realizing I wasn't
puzzled exactly but still not able
to articulate my thoughts—our walk in
the field now finished I just headed back

to the motel room and studied my shoes

Three Recent Trips to the Golden Past: East Village, Clarksdale, Athens

for Emmett Jarrett

this year I was excited to find the
DeRobertis pastry and coffee shop
still just where I left it—First Avenue
near Tenth Street—in the late 1960s

at the Delta Blues Museum I saw
the cabin where Muddy Waters was a
child on Stovall's plantation—it's not known
how often he came back for a visit

in Athens I walked through the Agora
where the ancients shopped   gossiped   argued   sent
slaves on errands   and male citizens met
for democratic decision making

     * * *

in the pastry shop I felt right at home
those were good times—yes a sentimental
and foolish observation but this coffee
always turns me happy and shortsighted

and without sentimentality where
would we be? one Clarksdale hotel offers
sharecropper shacks refitted with indoor
plumbing and central air conditioning

I loved the Parthenon and tried to shake
off the fact that it wasn't Phidias
who hauled all that marble up the hill   how
long does it take to forget slavery?

＊＊＊

let me get this straight: 58,000
dead Americans   plus Vietnamese
Mark Clark and Fred Hampton killed by cops and
I'm nostalgic about the espresso?

so much depends on your point of view: should
the Mississippi state flag retain its
Confederate stars and bars? just this year a
voters' referendum resolved the question

one Agora vendor sought sympathy
from a jury with the claim that he was
so poor he owned no slaves—about this time
democracy in Athens was reaching its peak

A Story About Desegregation

When We Were Young

"there" says Robert pointing to a second
floor window as we drive past Clarksdale High
"chemistry lab my junior year   I stood
right there and saw those kids on the sidewalk"

and thirty years later   in this August
heat wave   his memory is clear—students
from the black school across town standing in
front of the high school   a silent demand

that the schools obey the court order to
desegregate—young Robert opens the
window and calls out "what do you want" "we
want to come in"   he smiles and waves his arms

"well then" he says "come on in!" instead—as
local custom dictates—the police just
throw them in jail for awhile: they keep on
singing "nobody's gonna turn us around"

A Great Meal

at lunch Robert finishes his story:
the schools did integrate soon after that
though the two sides of town remain somewhat
separate   it's a good story   almost
as good as the cabbage and cornbread here
at Eugene Hicks' grocery store and
barbecue where Bill Clinton (craving some
soul food) ate during his "poverty tour"

—note: Clarksdale is still poor—and now Mr.
Hicks   refusing to charge us for our lunch
says it's "leftovers"   this is that Southern
hospitality I used to take lightly

Rashomon

while we're discussing 1970
the owner's brother stops by to chat and
offers "do you want to know what really
happened that day?"   at the time he owned two
old buses to supplement his job at
the supermarket meat counter so he
was the one the Clarksdale NAACP called
when they needed someone to take those kids

across town to the high school and that night
he drove across town again to fetch them
from jail   "soon as we crossed the bridge" he says
"we could hear them singing"   so the story
has a new ending   he adds that when word
got out about who drove that bus a white
co-worker at the meat counter said "James
"you're going to get a knife in the back"

From the Outside

this is when—either suffering from the
August heat or high from the cabbage and
cornbread—I get dizzy just trying to
fully integrate my tour of Clarksdale:

Eugene Hicks' photos of Bill Clinton at
lunch and the Secret Service business cards
framed on the wall by the counter   "if you
come to DC   Mr. Hicks   just call us"

young Robert who grew up to be a fire
department captain   James Hicks who could have
been killed for driving that bus   is instead
a city commissioner   Robert smiles

again and says "yeah now I work for him"
then I remember that you have to mash
the cabbage into the cornbread till they're
thoroughly mixed and that's what makes the flavor

The Camel Chronicles, Continued

Act II: An Actual Race Is Proposed

*"Contention continues in the early
morning hours of our fair city in the
little café on Highway 61,
the Rest Haven"   so the second act starts:
the dispute is still simmering the next
day over grits   biscuits   eggs and bacon
when Chamoun and the Preacher come into
focus as the story's chief antagonists*

*the Preacher   impatient   says he'll get a
horse   and dares Chafik to find a camel:
"got one already" he says   pointing to
the stuffed camel on top of the glass pie case
to which the Preacher says "get serious"
he wants to settle things with a real race
but again the tolling bell beckons him
and this time on the way out he passes*

*"self-appointed but never elected
mayor of Clarksdale" Jimmy Walker (who
also happens to have donated the
stuffed camel)   and the Preacher's parting shot
is an admonition that he should help
Chamoun find a real flesh and blood camel
to which Walker quips: "Republican or
Democrat?" a setup for the Preacher*

*who says "I was told Republicans don't
have blood" a great exit line   and a good
joke for insiders no doubt   certainly*

a nice twist to conclude the episode
but there's more: first an on-line vote: you can
register your views in the space below
on which is faster   camel or horse   then
some international funny business

where Clarksdale's "ambassador to Norway"
Grady Palmer   phones the Mayor   offers
to open an embassy in Oman
(you may recall the whole thing started there)
and Chafik's "gambling buddy" Doyle Varner
says he'll get a camel   but recently
he's had problems with some Iranians:
transactions involving equipment for

cotton gins have not gone well so—as Chafik
reminds him—the guys looking for Salman
Rushdie may be after him too   which gives
Doyle some second thoughts about his offer

* * *

theoretically these *Chronicles*
might have been read on the Web by millions
even less qualified than I am to
comprehend Clarksdale Mississippi   what
could they have thought   did horse partisans
from Texas log on   was there outrage from
sheiks not known for their appreciation
of Delta humor   did the *Chronicles*

hear from Salman Rushdie's attorneys   were
unamused ayatollahs calling for
maps of Mississippi   and how many
of the world's literal minds took this rare
opportunity to express their views
on line   this does raise the stakes: Clarksdale is
not just cognizant of the world but now
sets out to pull the world's leg   a big tease

Rhetorical Interlude in Three Stages

1. disclosure

now I think it's time for some disclosure:
visiting Clarksdale once or twice a year
I seldom went to Chamoun's Rest Haven—
since there was always the motel breakfast

and after a mid-morning snack (Delta
Donut) I'd be mostly downtown for lunch
from the takeout catfish place or eating
at Sarah's Kitchen   blues playing on the

radio   and blues posters on the wall—
as for the rest   beans coleslaw and a slab
of ribs from Mr. Hicks would last for at
least two suppers   so I was quite content

and immersed in blues—if Clarksdale is a
pond I dropped like a stone toward its very
center   which is blues   and for a long time
it was only there I wanted to be

but the ripples do spread: before blues there
was cotton   white crop nursed by black slaves   and
before that the settlers who cleared out swamp
forest   indians   and after cotton:

the war   the New South   the town   more cotton
the railroad   prosperity   immigrants
Jim Crow   war again   flood   depression   war
again   machines that pick cotton   ripples

spreading around me as I try to sink
deep into Clarksdale   so while I revel
in blues   the way I have shared in them here
I'm looking for more   obsessed with Clarksdale

talking to friends   mining the library's
old newspapers   seeking to understand
how people awash in this history
have managed now to live together here

because—as much as a stranger can—I
felt the life of the blues community
but outside of it were all those other
Clarksdales I could not find a way into

until these *Chronicles*   these inside jokes—
of farmers   merchants   businessmen   lawyers
the church culture   the City Hall crowd—set
in this place where they all act like themselves

2. context

and all this reminded me of Athens:
we had climbed the Acropolis to see
the Parthenon of course but then went down
to the Agora—ancient marketplace
where for a thousand years citizens   slaves
foreigners   vendors   idlers   travelers
did their business   stopped in at the temples
ate   drank   argued   shopped   lived their public lives

the evidence—dug up   pieced together
and displayed at the small museum there—
includes scratched or painted graffiti on
clay pots   or just fragments   a booklet notes:
"such...communications and expressions
of individuality achieve...
importance by virtue of their very
triviality. The writers, intent

on their own concerns...giving no thought to
the searching eye of history, reveal
themselves unselfconsciously and give us...

46

insight into everyday life…" so we
have been given these *Camel Chronicles*—
equivalent to—for instance—"…put the
saw under the threshold of the garden
gate" scratched on a shard found with two vases

both inscribed—in an Attic lettering style—
"I am Thamneus's"   but the letter
forms and dialect of the shard's message
suggest it was written by someone else
maybe a neighbor (and probably from
Megara near Corinth) either asking
to borrow the saw   or telling Thamneus
how to give it back   the booklet contends

that the language is really "too curt" to be
a polite request for a loan   so more
likely it was the Megarian's saw
and it's "easy to imagine" him just
leaving town hastily to "visit a
sick grandmother in Megara" but then
(thinking the guy who borrowed his saw may
not know how to return it to him)

the anxious (or conscientious) neighbor
grabs "a handy potsherd"   scratches his note
flags down a passing small boy and sends him
off to deliver it to Thamneus
(this is why when exploring the life of
the ancient Greeks you must always be sure
to visit the Agora as well as
the Parthenon)   and—is this a joke in

Camel Chronicles style?—a plain water
jar seems to parody the fancier
prizes awarded to the winners of

athletic games   with the inscription   "as
for that Olympic victor Titas   he's
always primed and hot for sex"   and on a
bigger jar: "cheap wine"   well maybe but in
Greek that's also the word for "vinegar"

and on a small shard: "Eumelis, come as
fast as you can. Abresimos" and—a
love note?—"Alkaios seems beautiful to
Melis"   and what looks like a shopping list:
"(kneading-) trough / long loaves (20) / oil flask   bowl
dishes: middle-sized platters (4)   little
dishes (5)   cups (2)" and another from
800 years later   though this one might

instead be a list of expenditures:
"pine cones   buns   fish or relish   peaches   freight
charges   fish or relish   wine"   and this is
why when exploring the life of Clarksdale
you must be sure to visit the Lily
Pad Gift Shop   Kroger's   Abe's Barbecue   Wong's
Foodland   Econo-Lodge and the Up-Town
Motor Inn   Conerly's Shoes   as well as

the Chamber of Commerce   the Delta Blues
Museum   and the Carnegie Public
Library   you must find music at Red's
and Messenger's as well as Ground Zero Blues Club
and Hopson's and you must
understand how crucial it is to pay
attention to the *Camel Chronicles*
as well as the *Clarksdale Press Register*

3. peroration

have I digressed? of course I finally
did go to Chamoun's   soon after starting
this poem   years after the *Chronicles*

48

ended (though—as you know—I contend that
they're as much with us as ever) I had
an excellent breakfast then introduced
myself to Chafik Chamoun   explaining
what I was up to and showing him my

first few pages which seemed to amuse him
and sure enough some of those I knew as
characters were there having coffee so
I began to feel like a character
myself in one of those novels where the
protagonist who has the same name as
the author is writing a novel he
can't finish with the same name as the one

he's in himself   if you see what I mean:
the place was more real but less vivid than
the *Chronicles* I'd been reading   so my
sense of "fiction" blurred around the edges
as Chafik took me over to meet Grady
Palmer   (still a city commissioner):
the seed of the embassy joke was his
visit to Notodden   Clarksdale's sister

city in Norway   which also holds a
summer blues festival every year and
I love this casual linking of the
"Blues Clarksdale" and the "*Chronicles* Clarksdale"
because it's this connection that holds the
city together   but—since I've digressed
enough already with all the old Greek
graffiti—I will just shut up for now

❋

Where Conversation Never Ceases

So Italian

1

Fabrizio Poggi   Italian master
of the blues harp   in Clarksdale this week—one
stop on his lifelong pilgrimage—has joined
us for lunch   and I'm showing him this book
I've come across   *The Delta Italians*
labor of love for a retired priest who
grew up down the road in Shaw   tribute to
his people "descendants of Italian

immigrants who settled in the Arkansas
and Mississippi Delta" starting in the late
nineteenth century as sharecroppers and
tenant farmers on cotton plantations
where   like the blacks   they soon found themselves in
deep peonage—"disease, inadequacy
of medical [care], exorbitant cost
of…provisions, low rates of wages, lack

of drinkable water…ill treatment by
and dishonesty of the bosses" (more
than seventy killed by yellow fever
in one year)   when Fabrizio reads this
page he lights up like the neon beer sign
at Red's juke joint   "of course   of course!"   he's so
excited his English nearly fails him
he's been struck by his own spiritual

recognition: it's this shared history
these linked racial memories of blacks and
Italians both suffering in the Delta
that account at least in part for his life as
bluesman   his Italian deep soul and blues heart

2

Agostinelli Angeletti Alpe
Antici Antone Arseo Bagioli Balducci
Baioni Barbieri Borgognoni Belvedresi
Brunini Canonici Camarato
Campassi Camponova Cardetti
Cavallo Ceranti Cesare Cirilli
Clerico Correro Corso Costatini
Curcio DeMarco Demilio
Donzelli Eusepi Fabri Fava
Ferracci Ferri Fratesi Gabucci

Geraci Giacelli Grego Liberto
Lubiani Luzietti Malvezzi Mosco
Morisco Malatesta Malavasi Marinelli
Mandolini Mangialardi Marascalco
Morgantes Noe Nicolini Oldini Pagnini
Perini Pasquellini Petretti Radicioni
Reginelli Rico Rizzo Rocconi Romagnoli
Rosatti Rossi Sabbatini Santini Santucci
Sbravati Serio Spaccarelli Spiva Tarzi
Tavoleti Tuminello Tocacelli
Vetrano Vitale Zavatta Zepponi

Some stayed   some quit   some bought their own farms   some
opened groceries   stores   small restaurants
in his book Father Canonici writes
their family histories   at the end
he notes that his next effort will be a
cookbook called *So Italian*

3

the Campassi brothers Louis Joe and
Silvio came through Ellis Island to
Clarksdale where Louis Junior was born in
1918   grew up: in the house (where

they had grape   blackberry vines   apricot   pear
scythe for cutting grass "you could shave with it")
and in the store on Issaquena
"If you couldn't find it at Campassi

Brothers, you couldn't find it. You just as
well quit" says Louis   clothes   shoes   and those blues
records because "my brother Willie was
crazy for the blues"   in fact persuaded
Uncle Silvio to "run a wire from
the loudspeakers over the store down to
his Savoy Theater so the blues would play
in the background of the silent movies"

(something again deep in the Italian
soul: Fabrizio are you listening?)

Barbara Borgognoni says when she and
Paul make sausage at home all seven grown
children still come to help although today
they don't start with their own hogs and the
grandfathers are no longer here to make
the "best wine I ever drank" says Paul   who played
high school football back when Italian boys
were welcomed as power fullbacks or star

"speed merchant" halfbacks—Paul ran one kickoff
back 85 yards to score   he could pass
and kick too   though these boys didn't play much
tennis at the Clarksdale Country Club—no
Italians (Jews   Chinese   blacks) need apply—
living just outside of town Paul and his
brothers went to Friars Point High School where
each season he would lead the team to a
lopsided victory over Clarksdale

Dorothy Antici Middleton tells
me about her grandfather Antici's

youth in Italy   "his job was to go
pick acorns up off the ground   frozen   he
would have to pry them up   they'd make acorn
bread   hard as a rock but it would be all
they had to eat" yet as an old man he
talked of Italy "fields   grapes   olive trees

the landscape he missed tremendously"   both
memories   I reflect   so vivid in
his mind   as if Italy were two kinds of dream

4

a century after the Italians
first came to the Delta (on a ship called
the *Chateau Yquem,* Father C tells us)
the Tarzi family of Clarksdale
runs a small restaurant that reminds me
how one historian called the Delta
"the most Southern place on earth"   and strolling
down Delta Avenue   walking into

Delta Amusement I'm sure this must be
it—the way a slow-paced morning unfolds
from early breakfast to coffee break (how
many years have these same men been coming
here?) to plate lunches served in the cool dimness—
a historian would also take note
of these clippings about Clarksdale sports on
the wall: in most of them Jimmy Tarzi

and his brother Attilio (who still greets
customers—his son Bobby is in charge
of the place) presided like the great law-
givers and judges over generations
in Clarksdale as refs and umpires   they have
been at the center of something crucial
but Jimmy and I are not talking sports now:
I've told him I'm writing poems about

Clarksdale   Jimmy says that during World War
II in France heading for the front he wrote
a poem himself—"Train of Death"—then months
later the war's over   he has survived
and is on his way to Clarksdale not as
an immigrant but as a soldier coming
home   so he adds two final verses:

as the train moves into the darkness of night
then comes the morning light again
I know then

it is not the train of death I ride
but the train of life
the train of the future
the future of America

5

Coda

I was feeling it all   such history
warmth   energy   persistence through hard times
reading Father C's book   talking with these
Clarksdale friends   being with Fabrizio
at his great awakening   I wished for
some revelation   some connection of
my own with this story   I am after all
a blues musician too   but of course I'll

never be Italian   and it never occurred
to me   meditating thus   that Father
C might be able to perform what—for
me at least—seems a miracle   turning
to the Clarksdale section of his book (late
very late   reading in bed after a
jam session at Red's) I find Father C—
unfamiliar with Clarksdale—has been told that

he's likely to find farmers   Italian
and otherwise eating breakfast at the
Rest Haven restaurant   he looks around
"to see if I could spot someone I knew
or someone who at least looked distinctly
Italian"   but failing in this he concludes
that in Clarksdale "the Italians had blended
into the general population"

and he reflects: "in most parts of the Delta
everyone looks more or less alike" then he
wonders "who that different-looking man
was   he wore a Greek sailor cap and a
black jacket with 'POET' in large pink letters
on the back" what?   no   yes   that's me   I was
eating breakfast in Clarksdale   he is seeing
me! and this is Father Canonici's

small miracle: long before I'd even
thought of writing this poem he has put
me in his book   or have I fallen asleep
and dreamed this   no   I'm awake   but feeling
like Aristotle is at my shoulder:
"hey poet with the Greek cap   you've got it
going here   these voices   your harp player's hot ecstatic
blues epiphany (so Greek dramatic!)

the soldier who recapitulates his
ancestors' journey (a classic structure)
then you turn up as a character yourself
all this demonstrates my theory that 'art
imitates life'"   but then I felt a tap
on my other shoulder   it was Oscar
Wilde saying: "no my friend   that's precisely
backwards—on the contrary   here you are

lying awake in Clarksdale reading about
yourself in Clarksdale   and tomorrow morning

58

after breakfast at the Rest Haven you've
arranged to meet the priest who wrote the book:
this all proves beyond a doubt the truth of *my*
notion that 'life imitates art'!"   I was
uncertain which to believe but then I
thought maybe I could say yes to both

The Wisdom of "Pap" Pang
Or
Typecasting in the Delta

I. Prologue

if all those stereotypes about blacks
are the most pervasive   tough to root out
and probably most damaging in the
historical long run   there's no shortage

of close seconds—like our Western view of
the Chinese: some of the Charlie Chan movies
offered us two for the price of one—his
black chauffeur   (the big eyes   the "yassuh" grin)

plus Charlie himself   cool crime-solver (in
spite of help from his son)   and those of us
of a certain age fondly remember
his faux-Confucian proverbs   "owner of

face cannot always see nose" or "shot in
dark sometime find eye of bull"   and there's that
most venerable of stereotypes—the
"yellow peril incarnate..." Doctor Fu

Manchu who embodies "the cruel cunning
of an entire Eastern race" almost like
genial Charlie's evil twin   indeed
early on they were portrayed by the same

Swedish-born actor Warner Oland—you
may have observed that they were never seen
in a film together let alone the
same room—Oland also appears in *The*

Jazz Singer as Al Jolson's father (you
want types? this is a very Jewish type)
is there a joke here about typecasting?
let's just acknowledge the power of an

image to obscure history   to shape
fact   even to repudiate fact and
in the end to appear as the simplest—
and most credible—explanation for

the most complex realities   human
character for example: take one of
my favorite Steinbeck passages from
his Monterey stories   where Mack tells Doc

that their local Chinese grocer has left
town unexpectedly—puzzling this out it
does seem to come down to the mysteries
of character: "there never was a friend

like Lee Gong" says Mack   Doc agrees: "yes he
was wise and good" "and tricky" says Mack   "and
smart" adds Doc "they volleyed Lee Chong back and
forth" observes Steinbeck "…out of their memories

there emerged a being scarcely human,
a dragon of goodness and an angel
of guile. In such a way are the gods created."
Mack's conclusion: "You can't never find out

what a Chink's got on his mind. . . ." sly Steinbeck—
to raise the old specter "inscrutable"
and then reserve the last word for himself:
"who could have suspected the secret

turnings of his paradoxical
Oriental mind which seems to have
paralleled the paradoxical
Occidental mind."

II. History

and speaking of the Occidental mind
and its paradoxes   have you heard the
one about the Chinese in the Delta
who (some of them) married blacks   leading to
the problem that you sometimes couldn't tell
if the child who *looked* Chinese was mixed-race
so some white Delta schools in the old days
of separate-but-equal had to bar

Chinese altogether   though in other
cases that had already been done (and
don't ask me why but what suddenly springs
to mind is an old punch line   something like
 "that's funny   you don't look Chinese"   no   it's
the New Yorker visiting Peking: the
Chinese rabbi says "that's funny you don't
look Jewish")   here's another   though very

different in tone   and for this one you
need the setup: right after the Civil
War   during Reconstruction   black labor
for understandable reasons was more
scarce than it had been   capitalists
and planters met in 1869 in
Memphis   formed a joint stock company to
bring in Chinese "coolie" labor   that is

workers from China but also some who
were already in California or
building railroads across the West: and in
their planter/capitalist/Western minds
the Chinese "coolie" stereotype—dumb
stoic peasant (and blessedly passive!)—
must have seemed just what they needed   here's the
punch line   from an encyclopedia

a true masterpiece of understatement:
"the Chinese did not adjust well to the
Mississippi plantation system"   as
if it were some cultural problem they
just couldn't work out   thus in the Delta—
where most of them were—the Chinese became
merchants   grocers   brought families over
from China   sometimes had their own schools   their

status in this respect was dealt with in
1927 by the US
Supreme Court itself which ruled the intent
of the 1890 Mississippi
Constitution to be clear when it says:
"separate schools shall be maintained for children
of the white and colored races" (which would
seem to settle the Chinese/black problem)

and "yellow, after all" as one account
puts it "was a color"   but it was not
black   so for this (I surmise) and other
reasons—for one thing China was
our ally in World War II—the Delta
towns   gradually   let Chinese children
into the white schools unless "anyone
objected"   the small Chinese groceries

(where as a rule the families also
lived) were mostly in black neighborhoods "for
business purposes…but [we] went to school
with whites" as one man recalls   "we had to
become adept at balancing between
blacks and whites. We were…allowed into both
worlds, but we mainly stayed among ourselves.
We were in both worlds but not of both worlds."

III. I Meet Pap

talk about irony   grim humor   you'd
expect the Delta Chinese to have some
appreciation for the fine points   thus
meeting Lin "Pap" Pang I should not have been
surprised to find a patriarch full of
laughs (and a few of them at my expense)
as well as history   here's a man born
in the Delta whose father sent him and

his sisters and brothers to Hong Kong for
three years to learn the language ("a Chinese
that can't speak Chinese" Pap's father said "is
not Chinese")   who trained World War II Navy
pilots in flying blind with instruments
came home after medical discharge and
two years in the hospital to work and
farm—Pap bought land   then buildings in town   made

money   when I told Robert—always my
guide—I wanted to talk to someone in
the Chinese community he said Pap
one of the wise elders for sure   would be
full of stories   wisdom   gossip (though he
failed to mention jokes)   Pap shares a house with
his niece and nephew Sally and Gilroy
Chow not far out of town   Robert called Pap

and he was waiting for us—slight and
looking quite spry I thought for ninety-two—
Robert introduced me   we sat around
the table   later Gilroy came in too
I should have known I was in for it when I
asked Pap first if it was OK with him
for me to record our interview and
his response was "if it's OK with me?

what can I do if you didn't tell me?"
(uncanny resemblance: that old Jewish
joke "why does a Jew always answer a
question with a question?"   punch line: "why not?")

IV. Two Interviews

I knew from my reading that the Chinese
in the Delta and elsewhere in the South
had not developed "Chinatowns" as in
the more urban North and West   so I asked
Pap what had kept the community
together—he said another Chinese
guy called him once "after I got on my
footing" with a challenging question: "Pap"

he says "the Jews got an organization
the blacks got an organization   the
Italians got an organization
how come the Chinese don't have one?"   and Pap
rising to the challenge   confers with three
other leading Chinese businessmen   "we
ain't going to depend on…donations"
says Pap   "we'll foot it"   and so they buy a

building   it's the "Chinese-American
Association"   big social events
seven or eight hundred people: sit-down
banquets which far outweighed formal meetings
and though such golden days are gone   there are
still Chinese in the Delta and here in
Clarksdale—merchants   professionals   all kinds—
even if the sense of community

has changed: "at one time" Pap recalls "it was
a novelty to see a Caucasian
marrying a Jew   Italian   Chinese
or whatnot   but now it's so prevalent

you have to look real hard..."   meaning I think
that Pap sees truth in the proverbial
melting pot metaphor   he does make a
shrewd guess about me though: "are you Jewish?"

"yes"   (note that I did not answer with a
question)   this takes us to Memphis where young
Pap before the war rented from
a Jewish landlady   and then to role
reversal   "I'll tell you a fair question
let me do the interviewing"   "OK"
"what's your daddy do" "he was a social
worker"   "how did the Jewish people come

to the United States"   pause   Pap observes
charitably "you ain't that old"   I try
anyway—the peddlers and businessmen
back in the 17th century   then
the biggest...warming up I start toward
the Enlightenment   the later pogroms—
but Pap cuts to the chase   "and how'd they get
in the dry goods business?"   a longer pause

"I think similar to the Chinese...they
came...some of them were itinerant..." (Pap
gives me the interviewer's "mm-hmm") just
going around the countryside selling
and then they got into businesses..."   this
is too slow for Pap   who's reminded of
a story: "do you know what BVD
means in underwear?"   very long pause   "no"

he turns to Robert   who makes a valiant
effort "I've heard of it"   but no   we're both
uninformed on this one   Pap explains that
his family had Jewish neighbors ("we
called him Papa Lipson") with a store where
one day "this little white boy...came up there

66

to buy BVDs   he says 'what's this mean
BVDs?'   'I can't tell you   I only

sell it'"   the boy (is he suspicious?   just
fooling around?)   says "then I don't want it"
Papa Lipson   thinking fast   says "I'll tell
you what it means   then you'll be satisfied:
it means Button Vay Down"   of course you had to
be there—not at Lipson's but together
with Gilroy and Robert drinking green tea
in that neat kitchen—to hear Pap's Jewish

accent   shocking and hilarious yes
but also familiar   Pap has a good
ear for it   and I thought I could almost
close my eyes and hear my Grandma Elsie

V. Pap's Farm

Pap's got punch lines all right but also more
subtle narratives   like the one where he's
just back home from the war   staying with his
sister   and finds a farm he'd like to buy—

five hundred good fertile acres—but he
comes up against * * * the rich and
well-connected cotton planter who has
set out to acquire the same place   Pap's no

match of course for this powerful figure
who is said to have claimed ownership of
"everything within forty-nine square miles"
and also to have cultivated an

image of paternalistic *noblesse
oblige*—giving out silver dollars to
his "hands" as they lined up in his cotton
fields—perhaps this is why   finding out that

young Pap recently back from the Navy
is also interested   * * *   makes
a gesture   sets up a meeting with Pap
and the agent one Saturday morning—

the big man (spiritual descendant
of those old stereotype-besotted
planters who pinned their hopes on Chinese labor)
has the self-assurance of one who can

afford to be magnanimous: "I tell
you what" he says "if Pap wants that land let
him have it if he got a down payment—
if he don't have a down payment" (after

what—sixty years? this seems a crystal clear
memory for Pap) "call Mrs. * * *
[the big man's secretary] she'll come up
here with it...I'm goin' to a ball game"

and Pap laughs at the transparency of
this ploy   * * * (he assures me) is
someone who "ain't *never* been to a ball
game"   and now of course since it's Saturday

(* * * has planned well) "all the banks were closed"
Pap crows   so the man can safely make his
magnanimous gesture then go about
his business   the agent (also a judge)

says "Happy" (this is his nickname for Pap)
"Happy   you hear what Mister * * * says   if
you want it he's gonna let you get it
but you have to have a substantial down

payment"   it's a game now   like poker   or
chess   or cat and mouse   so   as Pap recalls:
"we're BSing a little while...dinner
time he says 'I'm goin' home   if you get

here with some money you call me and I'll
come up here and give you a receipt' "Judge"
says Pap "like I told you before I have
intention of buying the land"   "Can

you get the money up?" "I repeat   I
came up to buy the land"   now Pap is
toying with the mouse   who is
perhaps doubtful   "you mean you can get up

some money today?"   "yes sir"   I watch Pap
relishing every moment   giving the
play-by-play dialogue   "Can you get up
and give me three   four thousand dollars?" "Judge

I repeat again I came up to buy
the land" "I tell you what   Happy" the judge
is a busy man "you go ahead get
your money   come up here   I'll come up here

give you a receipt" Pap says "Judge you don't
have to come back here   I got the money"
"You got the money now?" "yes"   "I reach in
my pocket and I say 'Judge give me a

receipt for twenty thousand'   I had twenty
one-thousand-dollar bills   'I hope that's enough'
'yeah yeah yeah I—I—I think so' (in Pap's
re-enactment the judge is heard stuttering

confused)   Pap laughs "he started worrying
about where he's goin' to put the money"
(you'll recall it is Saturday   all the
banks are closed)   "so he gave me a receipt

and I gave him the twenty thousand"   clearly
Pap—as Steinbeck might have put it—has
understood the paradoxical secret
turnings of the Occidental mind and

simply beaten his man—but why so much
more cash than was needed? Pap explains that
(perhaps under state law) a seller who
backs out after receiving such a down

payment is obliged to return twice the
amount—now Pap drives out to the land   telling
the farm manager "heard this place is for
sale" and he wants to look it over   only

to be told "ain't no need you wanting the
place—Mister * * * already bought it but
you can look at it if you want to" and
in courtesy he cautions Pap about

driving in the fields: "stay on the turnrows
because you get off you might get stuck back
there"   to which Pap   equally courteous
replies "thank you   I appreciate that"

VI. Inside Jokes

I love Pap's stories but I have been too
diligent in my reading not to try
out some amateur ethnography: "Pap
what's Chinese about your family and
what is Southern?"   "what's Southern? the Southern
part is specially when you Northerners
come up here and get a kick out of me
speaking with a Southern accent   y'all think

it's something odd"   so much for dilettante
ethnographic research   but this does give
me the chance to tell my one Southern joke:
New York guy visits the Delta around
Christmas   goes to see the local pageant—
all comfortingly familiar except
for the Three Wise Men dressed as firefighters
he inquires later as to this detail

"you Yankees don't know much—it says right there
in the Bible the Three Wise Men came from
afar"   this one's a hit   and there's one
more I'm trying to recall but just then
Pap says "I'll tell you   instead of getting
into poetry writing you ought to
get into making these things here (plastic
placemats on the table in front of us)

"and it ain't going to take you all day
to make it"   "that's true   that's true" I admit
"writing a poem is harder than that—
takes me two or three days and nobody
pays me anything"   more conversation
while Pap is mulling this over   it's close
to the end of our interview and he's
thoughtful: "do you think poetry writing

pays off?"   "no   doesn't pay much"   "you Jewish
people are supposed to be among the
brighter people   and you're going to stake
money on a losing proposition—
I'd like to have met you" says Pap the shrewd
businessman "when I was..."   I've played this part
of the tape over and over but we
were laughing too hard for me to make out

the rest   Pap's meaning had been clear enough
though   and what we were sharing was a rare
and hilarious Clarksdale confluence:
the Jewish poet from—it might as well
have been Mars—Pap the patriarch   Gilroy
the former NASA engineer   who as
a child left the Delta   lived in New York
but came back   Robert   local history

expert   fire department captain who grew
up here   his family old Clarksdale   who

71

never strayed far   who seems to me to know
everyone   and I have reflected on
just this moment: how is it I can be
so at ease in Clarksdale Mississippi
that I'm laughing at these jokes about Jews
and money right here—as my grandparents

would have said in Yiddish—in this room full
of "*goyim*" (wait: are the Chinese considered
goyim?) and I realize it's because
I'm hearing these as "inside jokes"   as if
we were all Jewish   and that is because
the four of us in fact are insiders
of one or another variety
and this afternoon what we've been able

to do is to consort as insiders
regardless of persuasion   then it strikes
me that—seen another way—insiders
are also outsiders   and we share that
as well—one more paradox perhaps of
the Occidental/Oriental mind
and this reminds me of my previous
thoughts on the logic of typecasting   the

grim pervasiveness of stereotypes
the power of the image   all of which
have—for now at least—lost some relevance
these past few hours   and I've remembered the
joke I was trying to recall just when
Pap started giving me career advice:
a very inside joke indeed that you
never tell when there are non–Jews around:

both from courtesy and to avoid your
own embarrassment—precautions that now
seem similarly much less relevant—
so I plow ahead with this joke that I've

72

always relished for its subtlety   the
levels of irony its punch line is
built on   telling it is in short a fine
way to close out the afternoon   and I

did consider including it here to
end this poem but it does seem to be
truly not for the general reader
on whom it might be wasted   I suspect
this joke—maybe like Pap doing Papa
Lipson—is a "you had to be there in
order to appreciate it" kind of
experience   or perhaps you would need
to be Jewish   or old Clarksdale   or Delta Chinese

Pinteleh Yid

1

why is it that my friend Elaine said once:
"the world is a Jew"?   something about the
human capacity for suffering
for absorbing pain   for endurance   for
laughter and of course for refusing to
surrender one's history   though sometimes
it can seem more like inability
than refusal   so that in Clarksdale   (where

as a blues sax player who visits twice
a year to hang out   play music with friends
I'm not especially Jewish)   I find
myself on Delta Avenue in front of an
old brick building that was once Beth Israel
("can a building cease being a synagogue?"
is I believe a different question
than "can a Jew cease being a Jew?") and—

though I haven't been in a synagogue
for years—here I am taking time out from
jam sessions   breakfast with friends   library
research on Clarksdale history just to
look at this building   and to reflect that
a hundred years ago   about when my
grandparents came from Russia to Brooklyn
there were also Jews already here in

Clarksdale—and to ask myself why   since I
am not much of a congregant nor a
great respecter of tradition   why it
is I am so moved by the story that
in 1911 here in Clarksdale

Mississippi a group of local
Jewish men—their names are not recorded—
went down to the railroad station where

a train had brought their new Torah   sacred
scrolls   and in procession they carried it
to this first temple   now derelict   old
white paint peeling off its brick façade and
modest arch (as in the old country): here
the Torah arrived   then   1918
some "prominent Jewish citizens" met
to prepare "plans for the erection as

soon as conditions permit, of a modern
and commodious house of worship" and
for "securing the services of an
accredited and competent rabbi"
(though it was still some years before Clarksdale's
second temple would actually get built
on Catalpa Street)   did this   I wondered
seem in 1918 like a big step:

to be planning a new holy place   did
Jews already see themselves as part of
the Clarksdale community   these downtown
merchants who thrived along Issaquena
Street   the "New World" district where WC
Handy once lived   where juke joints   cafés
and two movie theaters were scattered
among small stores   where (almost till midnight

on Saturdays) street and sidewalk were clogged––
shoppers   hucksters   kids   revelers   like an
ancient marketplace—and right in midtown
where the railroad tracks   as was the custom
separated the races   it was the
underpass on Issaquena that (as
it still does today) permitted easy
movement between the two sides of Clarksdale

so the Jewish merchants sold to black and
white   now the street is a ghost of itself
gradual victim like most of the town
of economic and social forces
out of its control   the stores boarded up
maybe one juke joint left on the corner
maybe a small restaurant where you get
plate lunches to go   but these are almost

as boarded up as the rest of them and
might or might not be there the next time you
pass by   at its height it must have been like
the Lower East Side   (one woman   we're told
would pull you into her store   grab a dress
and hold it under your nose "This here is
imported" she'd say "can't you smell the ocean?")
even then they were not newcomers: these

itinerant peddlers who'd fled Russian
pogroms   Lithuania   Germany
had been settling here since 1870
some with families (names mostly gone now
judging from the phone book)   there are fragments
of transcribed oral history and no
single family is typical   but we
can piece together details about one—

the Kerstine brothers: Julius   (who bought land
from former Mississippi governor
JL Alcorn in the 1880s) Isidor
and Adolph   to whom John Clark the founder
sold lots on Delta Avenue: what would
become the first Kerstine residence and
store   this even before the city was
incorporated—as far as I can

tell from the oral histories this was
Adolph's department store   later passing

on to one of his three sons (also named
Isidor) who sold shoes and men's clothes: a
"haberdashery" in those old days   which
lasted into the 1950s   at
some point it was a jeweler's   today
abandoned   though around it signs of new

life on Delta   and here's a secret: if
you stop in front of the blank windows on
a hot Saturday as I did—maybe
a blues festival day   (so that what you
hear from the railroad station two blocks down
is music booming off the outdoor stage
not the train pulling in   Torah on board)—
and if you lift the grimy rubber mat

off the cement walkway into the store
there is "Kerstine's"   blue on white mosaic
tile   laid in by Adolph's hometown friend from
Germany   the baker who for a time
lived in the building   and you could think of
yourself trailing those Jews up Delta just
another two blocks to that first temple
across from the courthouse and not far from

Earl Brewer's house—who by 1918
was practicing law in Clarksdale after
his term as Mississippi governor
his three daughters grew up here   including
Minnie   the eccentric   who established
a Mississippi edition of *The*
Woman Voter   suffrage and progressive
periodical   and who in her teens

(according to the oral histories)
dated Adolph and Molly's son Caesar
so were the Jews indeed then part of the
Clarksdale community?   maybe   but on

the other hand we're told that Adolph and
the Governor "put their heads together"
to end the affair   wouldn't you like to
have been there   Brewer (who it seems was far

from the most bigoted leader of
Mississippi) with Southern-gentleman
courtesy perhaps   Adolph just ending
a long day at the store   "I certainly
appreciate your understanding Mister
Kerstine"   and neither Minnie nor Caesar
ever married   there's a Yiddish word for
matchmaker but what is its opposite?

2

in the documentary film *Delta
Jews* when a black man says of the Jewish
merchants in his small town that "you didn't
really expect them to do the same type
of things a white person would do" this is
meant as a compliment   a point that is
reinforced by an old photo of a
black woman clerk in a Jewish store: most

white merchants just did not hire black clerks   who
might for example inadvertently
touch a white person and were not likely
to be trusted with money   the Jews though
from the time they'd been peddlers had always
the narrator says   dealt with both whites and
blacks   and did not behave like most other
whites—thus these different expectations   but

they were caught like others in the civil
rights conflicts of the 1960s: a
rabbi talks in the film about the tough
dilemma those days had presented to

him and his congregation in a town
near Clarksdale: he is a refugee from
pre-war Vienna where a rabbi could
just leave   but those of his flock whose whole lives—

professions   businesses were rooted there—
could not   they stayed   not knowing of course what
was about to happen   this memory
stays with him as he angrily defends
his decision not to endanger his
congregation by speaking out against
the white power structure in such times when—
as Jews well knew—they could become easy

targets   understanding   one person says
that "it was not periods of calm and
prosperity they had to be wary
of   but times of turmoil"   thus it might not
have been a surprise when one influential
member of a Delta congregation
advocated joining the White Citizens
Council   reasoning that otherwise

the more excitable among those folks might
"begin to remember that we are Jews and
not Southerners and act accordingly"
and there was precedent: hate speech from the
Klan   bombings of Jewish buildings even
before this difficult period and
in Clarksdale   as elsewhere   young activists
from the North were not always welcome   while

those who were Jewish caused particular
discomfort for Beth Israel members who
as one said "felt like it put the Jewish
community on the spot"   and if some
of them came to Friday night services

"people I can't say were really gracious"—
and though I see   as the film's narrator
says   that the Delta Jews knew only too

well how "social upheaval had a way
of unleashing resentments" and thus felt
they must protect themselves   still this troubled
me   on the other hand some Clarksdale Jews
with ancestral memories of pogroms
and holocaust were "very in favor"
when black and white activists fought hard to
start up the county's anti-poverty

program and keep it going (against strong
bitter opposition)   and the bank that
gave loans to poor blacks was the one with the
Jewish president   David Califf   in
any case the Jews faced some hard choices
and I thought the dramatic climax of
the film was exactly this crisis of
identity—which they survived   although

like the rest of the Delta they still faced
economic decline   businesses and
stores were closing as more people left town:
in one Clarksdale scene a black man stands on
Issaquena Street   its boarded-up stores
behind him as he speaks   "the Jews in those
days" he says "had a relationship with
the blacks way beyond what they have today"

3

I wondered if anyone honored by
the Chamber of Commerce as Clarksdale's
Citizen of the Year had been Jewish
before Goldie Hirsberg in 2003—

80

but I couldn't figure out where to look
it up   just to ask around might have
seemed strange   and I think the point is that
probably nobody is keeping track:

that's one answer some hundred years later
to the question of whether Clarksdale's Jews
form part of the larger community:
they do   yet they have also retained their

identity—you can get one side of
that story from Goldie's husband George who
could tell you about the country club—
another side is to be found in this

encounter: the Hirsbergs   in a movie
theater lobby after the show   see
a business acquaintance from   as it happens
an old wealthy cotton family who is

aware of Goldie's latest project: the
drive for funds to keep the public library
open: no need to wait and discuss it
he says   then   evidently on sudden

impulse—leans against the building   writes out
a check for ten thousand dollars   "I think
he was deeply touched" says Goldie "by that
film"   what was it   of course it was *Schindler's List*

4

how I wish I had had the chance to meet
Abe Isaacson   who came from Russia in
1912 and lived to be 100
in Clarksdale   who made a living in his
store but who was really more the scholar
patriarch   philosopher   wise man and

writer   whose poem "Where the South Begins"
suggests an invincible good cheer   thus:

When you come to a land
Where everybody is a friend
Where, when you get off your train
Cordially, you are invited to remain
and *when you come to a land* where you can
farm   or open a store   where you'll find brave
men   *girls who are fair* with *more than their share*
of *virtue and charm*   then   in each stanza's

refrain: that's *where the South begins*   for
Abe Isaacson at least   but—for all that—
his memories of the old country   (told
in a manuscript on file at Clarksdale's
public library) yield tales so vivid
full of detail that it's difficult to tell
recollection from invention   so
we read that he grew up in Russia   or

Poland   that it was during his days with
the circus in Montana that he ran
into the girl he knew from Russia now
a fallen woman   that in his village
of Radoshkovitz one Passover they
were visited by a stranger who turned
out to be Elijah   that one childhood
friend grew up   came to America   and

turned out to be Al Jolson the famous
violinist   but the most wonderful is
the tale of Abe Isaacson's dream   in which
the Messiah comes to inform him that
"your Clarksdale members have gotten away
from the teaching of Moses"   they are   the
Messiah says   too "lazy to attend
services on Friday night" and on the

"most holy days" Rosh Hashanah and Yom
Kippur "they close their stores" only with some
reluctance   the Messiah himself tells
Abe Isaacson that "they don't deserve a
Messiah and perhaps they don't want one"
further   he says   "you are the one chosen
by me to lecture...those hard-headed
Jews to change.... But before you start on your

mission I will take you on a short
vacation to see and hear what the ten
tribes of Israel are doing in their
land where they were driven by King
Nebuchadnezzar" and sure enough Abe
Isaacson   in the company of
the Messiah   visits the lost tribes   trapped
as legend has it (and this dream confirms)

beyond the river Sambatyon   never
able to return home because
of its raging rocky torrent from which
it desists only on the Sabbath when
of course they cannot cross   he is given
a friendly welcome and asked where he is
from   someone takes "a large map" out of
a drawer and seeks—right here amid the

ten lost tribes and in the presence of the
Messiah himself—seeks without success
"to locate Clarksdale...no he could not find it:
there was Memphis, New Orleans, but not Clarksdale"—
obviously   as he remarks   thinking
back on the dream "it was not"   and is there a
touch of wounded hometown pride?   "it was not a
complete map"   Oh how I wish I had met Abe Isaacson

5

in the late 1930s Aaron Kline
says   when he came to Mississippi from
Lithuania there were perhaps a
hundred Jewish families in Clarksdale
the old Delta Avenue temple had
become the B'nai Brith lodge   the site of
meetings   dances and Sunday poker games—
as elsewhere: a Jewish community

social and religious   in fact there were
both reform and orthodox but they had
just the one Catalpa Street synagogue
so Friday night's liturgy would be mixed
and on High Holidays the orthodox
service was at 8 am   the reform at 10
orthodox again at 12 and both groups
together around 3 for the final

memorial service   all this part of
the inescapable adjustment   like
the need to keep your store open on the
Saturday Sabbath—busiest shopping
day of the week   maybe until midnight
so that if—as someone told me—you were
an orthodox Jew "you didn't need to
be in Clarksdale, Mississippi, because

you could not make it   you had to adapt"
or as Aaron Kline says   (and who should know
better than he in his ninety-fifth year)
"you know how the cycle of life goes   I
was raised orthodox in the old country
but you heard the saying 'when you are in
Rome you do like the Romans'   if you can't
make a *motzi* on a whole *challah*, you

have only half, you still can make a *motzi*
on the half—same blessing goes on a
piece that goes on the whole *challah*"   he'd come
first to Alligator   small farm town just
down the road where he joined his uncle and
a brother   married   moved to Clarksdale   his
own store   two children   widowed   remarried
retired   what was his business I asked   "they

used to call it *Yiddishe schmattes*   here
they called it dry goods   then they called it
'general merchandise'   you can't change the
nature of the grain: whatever it is
it is"   which also seems true of Jewish
Clarksdale where you had to stay open late
on the Sabbath   where you could get pretty
hungry if you didn't once in a while

eat barbecue   but where no one inside
or outside of the community doubted
that "a Yid is a Yid" as Aaron Kline
observes   adding that "they used to say in
Kovneh when I was going to high school
that the *pinteleh Yid*   if you have it
inside you can do a lot of things what
is not kosher, but the *pinteleh Yid*

the kernel of the thing   the main point   if
you have it you don't lose it that easy
you have the *pinteleh Yid* in you,
regardless where you go, what you do   you
can't take it away"   literally the
tiny point   the "Jewish spark" that seems to
have stayed intact all through his long journey:
"just lucky" in 1937

to get out of Lithuania he says
where "two years later, God forbid, the gates

were closed and the fires were all around. You
understand me what I'm talking about—
fire and water from all sides   Hell on Earth"
and despite almost sixty years in the
Delta   he still speaks with an accent that
could have just got off the boat   (or could have

belonged to my grandfather in Brooklyn
who kept the *pinteleh Yid* in his own
way   deciding at Ellis Island when asked to
fill out the proper forms that he wanted
to Americanize his name: he chose
"INTE"   his personal acronym for
"Intelligence   Knowledge   Truth to the End"
but he didn't know how to spell "Knowledge")

and now welcomed into Aaron Kline's house
even just talking in his dining room
I'm struck with this spark's persistence—it's been
a year since friends stopped by one Friday night
after services to say "Good Shabbas"
and to break the news that Beth Israel on
Catalpa Street a few blocks from his house
had been sold—the Jewish community

like the rest of Clarksdale was losing young
people to big cities or those with more
jobs   and as parents and grandparents died
and membership decreased   the synagogue
had to get by with visiting rabbis
for Friday nights and the high holidays
and then less frequent Sabbath services:
finally they decided (I was told)

that they would keep on as long as Aaron
Kline the oldest member could walk to the
synagogue   after that they thought   it would
be time to close up   and he'd been aware

this was coming but now it was done: "I
quoted them" he tells me "from the prophet
Jeremiah" about the destruction
of the first temple in Jerusalem:

"On all of this my heart cries   to see all
destroyed" in the prophet's words   and now the
selling of the synagogue   he says   has
broken his heart   which I believe   but it's
also clear to me that even though (like
Jeremiah) the heart may break   that old
stubborn *pinteleh* still glows and flashes
tough and luminous at the very core

6

those who grew up on Issaquena Street
Delta   or Yazoo   in their parents' stores
first or second generation born in
Clarksdale are now—many of them—about

my age   in their sixties   some have left   some
have remained   though few still work in the stores
Lawrence Magdovitz is an attorney
whose family came from Lithuania

which he visited after the war that
Aaron Kline so barely escaped: in the
Vilnius synagogue just a few old
men are left to pray every morning   in

Kovneh the Jewish cemetery is
now a soccer field   he tells me more of
Beth Israel's history in Clarksdale   the
community grew   eventually

acquired five Torahs   then the slow decline
then not enough families to keep things

going   and what happens to these sacred
scrolls when their work in this place is finished?

one of them went to a synagogue in
Poland   one to a camp for Jewish teens—
Lawrence himself has bought two   will give them to
a group that helps congregations just

starting up in the South "till they get
on their feet they'll have a Torah on loan"
and the last   which he also has   is "not
kosher" he says   old and in disrepair

to the extent that it's unusable
and technically he says it should be
put in a box and buried   but he may
instead give it to the Memphis rabbi

who has expressed interest: "what do you
want a non-kosher Torah for?" he asked
"you're orthodox"   the rabbi reminded him
that no one under thirteen is allowed

to read from the Torah   but this one   no
longer holy "I need" said the rabbi
"so I can teach the ones under thirteen:
it doesn't have to be kosher"   and one

of these five must be the Torah that came
here in 1911   now it goes
forth   isn't this   I'm thinking   some kind of
continuation—and Beth Israel's

cemetery is here of course   and the
two buildings that once were synagogues—all
this "of blessed memory"   and what else?
I ask Lawrence about Issaquena

Street   "it's too bad there's no map of all the
stores   which one was next to—" he interrupts:
"I know which ones were which" and then it all
pours out like one long sweet exhalation:

"starting at the corner you had Silvio
Campassi which was an Italian   then
you had Harry Laban's (whose son is a
doctor)   then you had a Syrian next
door that had a little café   the
Royal Café   next to that   a little
store   Herman Binder (whose brother was Leon
Binder who's now in Baton Rouge)   but he's

been dead for years   next to that was the Franks'
dry goods   across the alley from there was
the Hollywood men's store   fellow named
Marvin Bacharach   he was Jewish   the
Franks were Jewish   so was Herman Binder
next to that Sam Abrams had a little
dry goods store   next   a barber shop   then the
Hamburger Café   then next to the Hamburger

was Ben Jacobson's furniture store and
of course he was Jewish   next to that was
Al Israel's   he basically had a ladies'
store   a Jewish fellow   in fact he married
my mother's sister   next to him was Sol
Califf   (his sons and daughters live in Memphis)
next to them   Leon Binder   before him
was some people named Adels   next to that

was a little sundry drugstore   non-Jewish
then there was a sporting goods place and then
a five and ten run by an Italian
and then my father's store which was called Mack's
Department Store   next to that was a drug
store and on the corner was Kroger's   that

was on one side of the street"   what voice
I wonder   what force is speaking through this

matter-of-fact man   is he seeking to
rebuild something as lost as the Jews of
Kovneh?   now he's across the street: "then on
the other side   a Chinese grocery
then there was a liquor store   a little
furniture store   there were two little old
juke joints   next to that was Stetson's men's store
run by a guy named Irwin Shankerman

(his nephew runs the Shankerman's around
here)   next door to him   Irvin and Louis
Jacobson   they were Jewish   then there were
some more juke joints   then the next building was
Sol Kaufman's men's store   then the New Roxy
picture show   next to the New Roxy was the
Old Roxy and then it became Bacharach's
department store   and Ella Bacharach

who was the first Jewish girl born here she
ran it with her husband   next to that was
Abe May's department store   probably had
more stock and goods than anybody   a
juke joint next door and in the next building
was Morris Grover who was another
Jewish fellow   then across the alley
was the OK Grocery   and then the

Belmont Café which was similar to
the Hamburger: they had black on one side
and white on the other   next to that was
Mister Dave Auerbach's shoe shop   he was
a Jewish merchant   and next to him was
Simon Lurie   next to that was Victor
Binder   who had a store   and next to that
was Abraham Isaacson (his grandson is

90

Arnold Himelstein) then of course right on
the corner you had the Savoy picture
show which was run by Abe Aronoff   then
there were a few Jewish merchants over
there on Yazoo   Harry Baskin was
over there   Sam Schwartz   Abe Brooks was over
there   Hirsberg   he was an accountant   Fred
Cohen after he got burned out over

here on Delta he moved to Yazoo   the
Resnicks had two stores   Okun's shoe shop   we
had several doctors here   (Dr. Levy
Rubisoff   Foreman   Arick)   Isaacson
sold out   moved over here on Yazoo   sold
furs   bought furs and had a bookstore   you bring
two in   take one in exchange   he didn't
sell them   he accumulated one whole

hell of a lot of books"   by now I am
as moved   astonished   as when I first learned
of the Jews walking their sacred scrolls home
from the station   this immediacy
of life along Issaquena Street   told
flawless and vivid as Homer   now makes
me think that when I first stood in front of
the building on Delta Avenue what I

was failing to grasp is how   when faced with
surrendering one's history   the refusal
and the inability cannot always be
separated   which may be related
to the aphorism "it's easier
to take the Jew out of exile than to
take the exile out of the Jew"   and since
in my case it has turned out easier

to seek the *pinteleh Yid* in Clarksdale
than at home   it occurs to me that exile

is needed perhaps—like more darkness—to
see the spark   and I think that what I have
just been allowed to hear: Issaquena
Delta   Yazoo   as they were—all gone now—
as if Jeremiah were recalling
every detail of the Temple—this is

indeed a part of blessed memory
but beyond that it is the secret love
poem for Jewish Clarksdale   its own *Song
of Songs*   which   as the ancient rabbis have
told us   is among all others   the Holy of Holies

The Camel Chronicles, Continued

Act III: The Preacher Gets Mad, the Forces Gather, and the Race
Course Is Laid Out

five days later passions have not cooled   (so
much for those myths of relaxed Southern ease
and slow lazy climates)   a friend reminds
the Preacher that too much partisanship
from the pulpit on behalf of the horse
could be construed as political speech
thus breaching the wall between church and state and
threatening his tax exemption   to which

the Preacher responds in a rage "Damn the
IRS!…If the Bible says a horse
is faster I'm gonna preach it"   in a
corner booth James Hicks scrawls on his napkin
"John 3:16"   holds it up   the Preacher
opens his Bible to Jeremiah
4:13   "His horses are swifter than
eagles" causing Chafik to shake his head

"I dunn know. W'at you t'ink, Red?"   Bradham says
he recalls father Carol's Saturday
homily (from Psalm 33): "An horse
is a vain thing for safety: neither shall
he deliver any by his great strength—
Preacher" he adds "you don't know nothin' about
nothin'   all you do is sit there   read them
fancy books and play on your computer"

but again the Preacher has the last word
"You just get yourself a camel and put

your money where your mouth is"   meanwhile there's
action in several other quarters—
first we're given a startling look into
one character's mind: Jimmy Walker   whose
thinking—says the author—resembles that
of a well-known "representative of

the South—Br'er Rabbit…once a conniving
thought finds entrance it will not rest until
it devises a scheme advantageous
to his own welfare"   in this case Jimmy
is considering a "panorama"
of ways to make "the camel thing work in
Clarksdale: from building stalls in City Hall
to pastures behind the new county jail

while on the horse front the racing crowd in
rural New York state (according to one
local newspaper there) is outraged over
these camel claims: one champion trainer
and rider who's been in the Olympics
has volunteered to meet the challenge   and
at the track in Saratoga it's said
bookmakers are already placing odds

and now having reached the second week of
these Chronicles *(though it seems like years to*
me) it's been settled that the race will start
in the parking lot of the Rest Haven—
that is: on Route 61   South State Street
just over the bridge from downtown Clarksdale
near the new Hicks Barbecue   across from
motels   fast food   supermarkets   Wal-Mart—

and finish at Memphis's Peabody
Hotel   perhaps echoing the famous
dictum that the Delta begins in this
lobby and ends on Catfish Row in Vicksburg

Act IV: The Theory of Evolution Is Questioned, the Pope Weighs In, And Chafik Disappears

a spectator quietly eating his
kibbie and cabbage lunch at the counter
during one of the discussions this past
week   we're now told   is Father John Kerstin
who understands the clear implications
of this debate for the world's religions:
hurrying back to his office he phones
the Vatican   "Your Holiness" he says

"The Scopes Trial is about to be reversed...
Darwin's error about to be exposed!
...a race right here in Mississippi—horse
versus camel"   he's sure the horse can win
thus "proving once for all that God made it
a distinct and unique creation from
the Beginning"   to which the Pope responds
"I dunn know"   the camel   says the Pope   might

have evolved from the horse   and he observes
that in Christmas pageants it's always been
camels not horses: "no" he says "I think
the Church had better stay with the camel
and by the way" says the Pope "how's Chafik?
say hello to him and Louise for me"
hanging up he calls the Pontifical
Academy of Science together

to publish a decree: "New knowledge from
Clarksdale Mississippi" it says   "leads to
the recognition that the theory of
evolution is more than hypothesis"
the official position of the Church
is thus "that the camel is faster than
the horse"   naturally this announcement
riles religious conservatives worldwide

not to mention the Preacher—his sermon
the next Sunday blasts "false prophets" and "false
teachers" who try "to make believers saved
by grace go back to Old Testament Law"
no camels in the New Testament he
insists   except for the one passing through
that needle which was only for lack of
money   "all the saints"   he cries   "ride horses"

then "Repent! and your horses shall be white
as snow—Revelation 19:14"
is his big finish   causing several
"penitent saints" to swear they'll change their votes
but the big news is that Chafik has not
been seen for days   which however doesn't
alarm anyone   given his habit
of "feeding nickels to...those voracious

mechanical carnivores along the
Mississippi River" (one more inside
joke: casino slot machines)   shrugging
it off Louise says she's got "no clue"

* * *

it did take me awhile to follow the
logic: if you believe the camel is
faster and if being faster is
considered to be an adaptive trait

then the camel could have evolved from the
horse   ergo: evolution is proved and
the Preacher's fundamentalism
on this point loses (and so does the horse)

but surely the triumphant moment here—
and maybe the highest point so far in
these *Chronicles*—is the Pope asking to
be remembered to Chafik and Louise

every time I read it I laugh out loud
thinking about the old joke which   where I
come from   is told as a Jewish joke but
could just as easily be an Irish

Russian   Italian   or for that matter
Lebanese joke: on a passenger ship
to Europe Mr. Schwartz is annoyed at
his dinner companion   Mr. Goldberg

who is just a nice ordinary guy—
the annoying thing is how he seems
to know everyone   from the most
obviously rich high-class passengers

to the captain   who invites Goldberg to
his cabin for a drink and gives him a
special tour of the ship and so forth
so Schwartz is glad to arrive in Europe

see the last of Goldberg and head off on
his travels   which take him at some point to
Rome   one day he goes to St. Peter's Square
where thousands of tourists as usual

have gathered outside the Vatican and
suddenly there is wild cheering as the
Pope emerges onto his balcony
and—to Schwartz's astonishment—there's Goldberg

at the Pontiff's side waving to the crowd
just then a man standing next to Schwartz turns
to him inquiringly   "say   who's that up there
on the balcony with Goldberg?"   (or with

Sweeney   Popov   Giuseppe   or Chafik)
this goes way beyond Clarksdale connecting
with the world   or teasing   now the place wields
power and influence: the Pope himself

persuaded to act on this news from the
Delta and also eager to renew
acquaintance with his old friends the Chamouns—
the Vatican website by the way says

that the Pontifical Academy
of Sciences this year is having its
400th anniversary (in case
you were tempted to doubt the *Chronicles*)

I must say that—after all this—Chafik's
disappearance does not trouble me: no
doubt he'll be safe   in a story like this
any friend of the Pope is sure to win out

❋

Transformations

"Everything Reminds Me of My Dog"*

for TW and JO

*title of a song by Jane Siberry

when I heard that song "Everything Reminds
Me of My Dog" I thought it was funny
but also perceptive: it's not that things
literally resemble her dog but
that whatever else is happening the
dog stays on her mind   it's a sweet thought too
about a point of view that's thoroughly
determinist but also full of good

humor   until finally "this whole world
reminds me of my dog"   by contrast (and
by frightening similarity) I
was startled to suddenly recall the
scariest passage in *Moby Dick* where
Ahab reveals what everything reminds
him of: "All visible objects...are but
as pasteboard masks. But in each event...act . . .

deed...some unknown but still reasoning thing
puts forth the mouldings of its features from
behind the unreasoning mask. If man
will strike, strike through the mask!"   and since what he
hates is that "inscrutable thing" behind
the visible world   whether the whale is
the thing itself or its "agent...I will
wreak that hate upon him"   thus Ahab's mad

vengeance   such a grim joke when set next to
Jane's dog   that sunny embodiment of
grace and generosity toward the
world   and I wondered where I'd fit between
these extremes of single-mindedness   what
it is that I'd be unable to get
out of my mind   and then I was even more
startled to find that it's my visits to

Clarksdale where sometimes "everything reminds
me of race"   or rather it's the consciousness
of race   so maybe this consciousness is
part of the inscrutable thing behind
the mask   or else—also possible—my
Northern Jewish liberal mind is just
playing tricks with Clarksdale so that really
it's my own consciousness   in either case

there are days when indeed that is just what
everything reminds me of: the
public schools mostly black the private schools
mostly white   the black physician wishing
to join the Clarksdale country club:
most members said yes but—as the charter
stipulates—twenty-five "no" votes kept him
out   for some this was an issue (to quote

the *Press Register*) of the right to "choose
your own friends" which might equally be said
of the recent mayoral election
where the black Democrat beat out the white
Republican   in these enlightened times
this was not an upset or even a
big surprise—the only odd thing was by
how much the loser's total exceeded

the number of registered Republicans
and there was once I almost felt like the

mask had been stripped off—when a large local
institution hired a professional
person from out of state through resumé
references   phone interviews   it seemed
the process had been thorough enough but
too late they discovered they had gotten

a *black* professional person   so then
after some hemming and hawing there was
agreement that there would be no lawsuit
in exchange for a year's salary and
probably the avoidance of public
embarrassment at getting caught out—such
whiffs of overt racism are hard to
deny and harder to explain away

thus finally I'm not so sunny as
Jane and her dog—though I'm sure Jane has her
other moods as well—and sometimes I do
like Ahab wish I could strike through the mask—
though he   poor tormented soul   had no respite
from his quest—while I'm less self-destructive
and more practical   so whether what's there
is just my own consciousness or not I

have figured out that there are some ways
you can manage to mix black and white in
Clarksdale: often what you get then is blues
music   so I spend much of my time there
playing sax   blowing my brains out in jam
sessions where all consciousness can be at
rest and—except for an occasional
"what key?"—even words are not needed: I

glance across the stage and smile   for now at
least I don't think about the mask or what
might lie behind it and I never have
to ask these friends what everything reminds them of

Aaron Henry's Sandwich

*A handsome young Negro [Aaron Henry], dressed in slacks
and short-sleeve shirt, wiped his brow and addressed the
police chief, "Now look here, chief, there's no need in trying
to blow at us. Everybody scared of white folks has moved
north, and you just as well realize that you've got to do
right by the rest of us."*
—(*Autobiography of Martin Luther King, Jr.*, Chapter 23)

*Mr. Speaker, I rise today to honor a very special man and
a great American who has recently passed away. Aaron
Edd Jackson Henry, better known to friends and family as
"Doc," was born July 2, 1922, and died May 19, 1997.
Doc Henry's quest for equality took him across the Nation
and around the world. He was instrumental in enacting laws
that impacted the core of human rights in our Nation.*
—Congressman Mike Parker of Mississippi

*So I left Clarksdale a few pounds heavier from all of the ice
cream consumed at the old-fashioned soda fountain in his
Fourth Street Pharmacy but also many degrees uplifted by
the spirit and determination of Aaron Henry.*
—Congressman Sander Levin of Michigan

I. The Sandwich as Metaphor

if you visualize every life as
a sandwich   you could imagine endless
variations: with or without onions
hot   cold   lives sliced thin or just all mashed up

beyond recognition   the delicate
the familiar   the unsavory   crisp
or soggy   easy to chew but hard to
swallow   dry or absolutely perfect

a lunch to end all lunches   or a fast
food snack certainly best forgotten   and
so forth   from the long view of history
the "sandwich" of a particular life

might be seen as one crucial period
bounded by others less transformative:
an essential substance spread   squeezed   enclosed
between slices of "before" and "after"

this metaphor applies to the life of
a place as well: I think that for Clarksdale's
life and Aaron Henry's the crucial time is
the mid-nineteen-sixties when everything

changed because whites and blacks began—compelled
by history and themselves—to change their
behavior toward each other so that
from then on nothing was what it had been

Slices of Before

The city's slice of "before" starts where two Indian trails cross and
Europeans settle (the early 19th century). By 1850 the area has close
to three thousand residents, divided about evenly between whites
and black slaves. Cotton production, at the center of the economy,
has doubled in ten years, and cotton—in spite of all the floods, and
the destructive war—stays central for many years, though with new
problems, as foreseen, even before the war ends, by James Lusk
Alcorn, a prominent local planter (and later governor). He writes,
in 1862, "our negroes will soon be ashes in our hands, our lands
valueless without them."

But sharecropping comes to the rescue, and a railroad, which
helps Clarksdale thrive right into the next century. Still, though the
economy grows and changes, custom and social structures, abetted
by Jim Crow, remain pretty much in place for a long time.

1925 is the date of the last lynching in downtown Clarksdale, and
a history text written by local teachers in 1958 is likely to be (though

I'm guessing here) a reflection of the white community's general views: In this analysis Reconstruction is seen as a time when "public offices were largely filled by negroes, most of them incompetent" who "while [they] held office...terrorized the countryside" and when the former slaves "were taking a long holiday, but it was only temporary and they began returning to the plantations, begging for employment."

And (perhaps prophetic of white Clarksdale's response to what lay just ahead) these 1958 authors describe the time of their own great-grandparents, when the Northerners new to the Delta (the infamous carpetbaggers) came there "with no understanding of the land, the crop or the negro."

* * *

As to Aaron Henry's slice of "before": When he's born in 1922 near Clarksdale, his family is sharecropping. When he's five, they move off the plantation and a year later into Clarksdale, where he will spend the rest of his life. The young Aaron is a reader, a good student, who finishes high school and works to earn money for college. One white employer is kind, encouraging: "Get an education," though, as Henry remarks in a recent book about his life, "I doubt if it ever occurred to him that education would lead to my open discontent with the system."

In 1943 he is drafted into the army, assigned to a trucking division in Hawaii, and ends up more worldly—the army being slightly less segregated than Mississippi. Returning to Clarksdale in 1946, he finds "undercurrents rising to the surface," as groups like the Progressive Voters League are becoming more active. The GI Bill pays for his college, so he goes off to study pharmacy at Xavier University in New Orleans.

Four years later in Clarksdale, he and a white pharmacist, KW Walker, open the Fourth Street Pharmacy. Henry marries Noelle Michael and settles down to run the drugstore and work on civil rights in Clarksdale and all of Mississippi.

Inside the Sandwich

the sandwich is a flawed metaphor of
course—since "before" and "after" are not

106

detachable slices but involve cause
and effect—all metaphor is flawed in
that way though   never a perfect match   and
always threatening your command of it:
here I am seeking ways to focus you
on a complex history and I know

some literal reader is sure to be
reminded of lunch: "ah! chicken salad"
and the wise guys will ask if we shouldn't
include all the Mississippi police
of this era as a "*club* sandwich"   so
one does run into these problems   still   as
imperfect as it is you sometimes need
metaphor to impose clarity   shape

onto experience   life as we all
know—not to mention history or a
whole town—being contradictory and
cluttered   too often hard to make sense of
like Clarksdale in 1997:
my first visit   just a few months after
Aaron Henry's death—though I hadn't heard
of him yet—when I knew nothing of the

South   Mississippi   the Delta but the
history I'd read: bitter times   racial
struggles: instead I found a town full of
people being civil to each other
as if—to the eyes of a stranger—some
episodes from the past were no longer
visible   the way a mess of something
disappears beneath a neat slice of bread

                    * * *

1951 Aaron Henry notes
is a difficult year for Clarksdale blacks:
two teenage girls raped at gunpoint by white

men   and an epileptic youth shot dead
by police—no convictions—and he is
articulate in public about this:
three city officials come to the store
asking Henry's white partner to help

shut him up   but "I think Henry is right"
he says "and personally I would go
to hell for him" (let there be a poem
to celebrate KW Walker)
the Progressive Voters' League decides
to form an NAACP chapter
in Clarksdale   Henry becomes president
and   as elsewhere in Mississippi   change

comes   but slowly—in 1954
the state legislature moves to resist
the Supreme Court's school desegregation
decision   a year later Emmett Till
is killed in a nearby Delta county
for—they say—whistling at a white woman
he is fourteen   the NAACP
remains active in Mississippi

and in 1959 elects Aaron
Henry its statewide president   Freedom
Rides and sit-ins speed the pace of change   Ole
Miss is forced to admit James Meredith

                  * * *

on my visits I always stop in to
look over the new tourist brochures at
the downtown visitors' center which is
actually the old Greyhound station

on Third Street   recently restored   marble
floor   red and blue neon sign outside (the

famous galloping dog)   again the past
is there too   not quite seen but you feel it

somewhere underneath with its infamous
segregated waiting rooms here and all
over the South   and you wouldn't know that
here in 1961 Clarksdale had

its second sit-in of that year   (after
the one at the train station) or that the
Chamber of Commerce was then moved to bar
two black high school bands from marching in the

town's annual Christmas parade or that
this in turn sparked a black community
boycott of Clarksdale's white merchants led by
the local NAACP   or that

Noelle Henry was then fired from her school
teaching job and the next Christmas parade
was cancelled: to see all this you have to
lift that neat slice of bread off the sandwich

* * *

in 1963 when the mayor
will not discuss voter registration
schools   poverty   the black community
plans a mass demonstration in Clarksdale
they're starting out—as Henry tells it—and
the police chief suggests "Tell you what, Aaron,
before you march, how about letting me
take out some life insurance on you"   but

in the end the joke (was it a joke?) is
on the chief   since Aaron Henry will live
thirty-four more years   outlasting
the reigns of some few Clarksdale police chiefs
now   in retrospect   this is not a year

for jokes: JFK assassinated
and Medgar Evers in his own driveway
(after taking Henry to the airport)

and a young black man   twenty-one   shot dead
by Clarksdale police   accused (in Aaron
Henry's account) of trying to steal a
banana he runs out of the store   down
the alley but doesn't make it   and on
Good Friday someone firebombs Aaron
Henry's house   not a unique event by
any means but I think the first time that

the intended victim months later runs
for governor   in the unofficial
"Freedom Election"   ends up with more than
eighty thousand votes   demonstrating—as
Henry puts it—the inaccuracy
of Senator Eastland's smart remark that
Mississippi blacks are too lazy to
even register   then "Freedom Summer":

1964   Aaron Henry as
state NAACP president helps
organize the campaign to register
black voters   recruiting college students
to come south—like young Andrew Goodman from
Queens College who arrives in Clarksdale   spends
one night at his house and the next day heads
for Neshoba County to be murdered

with Michael Schwerner and James Chaney—two
months later the Mississippi Freedom
Democratic Party delegation
chaired by Aaron Henry tries to unseat
Mississippi's "regular Democrats"
at the national convention but the
last thing Lyndon Johnson needs now of course
in order to carry the South is to

let a bunch of black people represent
the Magnolia State: the national
party offers them two seats—it's not clear
how ready Henry is to compromise
but most of the MFDP group is
dead set against it   he says   and they all—
Aaron Henry included—feel betrayed
by their liberal allies   but the range

of reactions only serves to sharpen
the MFDP's internal struggles:
it has always been a coalition
of older and younger   liberal and
radical and grassroots   SNCC members and
others committed to direct action
the NAACP more focused on
legal remedies through the court system

and party politics   but the party
they are closest to has now weakened their
position—in the wake of this there's much
quarreling over future direction:
reflecting later Henry says he found
SNCC's ideas "frightening because they
were about something as foreign to the
American system as white supremacy…"

I think he means the separationist
tendency fostered by this betrayal
and then the black power movement: he will
never refuse to work with white allies

Keeping It Together

what Aaron Henry has helped to set in
motion is unstoppable now   though the
splits in the movement will widen and grow:
this time think how an overstuffed sandwich

needs that slice of bread on top to keep from
falling apart   so if his life were to
appear on the menu of history
as a "Mid-Sixties Coalition for

Civil Rights Action in Mississippi
Sandwich" Aaron Henry's slice of "after"
just now becoming visible serves to
hold things together—at least partly—(and

sometimes to cover disorder) I see
this time as "after" because it isn't
a transformative period but a
time of consolidation   where he's not

less active   far from it   but his role now
is largely to use the influence he
has been acquiring   predictably this
will sometimes bring him into conflict

with friends as well as with adversaries—
still   he persists: it's ten years since the Brown
decision and Clarksdale schools have not been
integrated—by 1965

the school district has come up with a "zone"
plan which—since neighborhoods are still pretty
much segregated—neatly manages to
change nothing   Aaron and Noelle's daughter

Rebecca is predictably denied
entrance to a school in the "wrong zone":   the
NAACP sues the district on
her behalf   Clarksdale is sent back to the

drawing board   as the district tries to come
up with a plan that will satisfy the
court's demands Aaron Henry remains
a force in weighing what's acceptable

for the black community (somewhere in
the midst of this   even before the final
settlement   a Clarksdale version of the
ubiquitous "private academy"

was established and still thrives while public
schools and most neighborhoods are nearly as
segregated—though *de facto* now—as
they were then—on the other hand the same

is true where I live in liberal New
England   but that as they say is a whole
other story   isn't it)   and it is
Aaron Henry who gets together with

some white allies to seek control of the
federal grants for Mississippi's large
preschool Headstart program—and they succeed
by ousting another bunch that Washington

views as dangerous radicals   Henry's
group—certainly not radical—takes
charge of the whole program   so what is this?
you could call it a retreat that weakened

the forces for political change in
Mississippi or you could say   as one
writer observed in 1991
that "those small yellow buses are [still] a

common sight…throughout the state"   and without
Aaron Henry there would probably be
no community action agency
in Clarksdale and Coahoma County still

running programs and employing people
throughout the county   then he's elected
to the state legislature where he will
represent his district for fifteen years

in these final years of his life the court
battles   struggles   arguments have not ceased
but no one's going to arrest him or
bomb his house   he's respected and he serves

honorably on behalf of his friends
and those who had been his enemies: there
are certainly some even today
who will tell you everything they didn't

like about his politics   his ideas
his personal life—but his importance
is not in question   which brings me to
the other sandwich I need to explain

II. Literary Digression

if metaphor helps to clarify and
shape experience   so does a symbol—
except that metaphor is a way of
thinking about something while a symbol
literally   concretely exists: it's
the thing itself—rather than "imagine
these lives as sandwiches" you'd have to say
"there actually *is* a sandwich here"

and metaphor (since it is a mental
image) knows no limits: so to picture
Clarksdale's life and Aaron Henry's as I
have done here I didn't need to set up

a scene in a restaurant—only to
sketch out some similarity between
a sandwich and the shape of a life   I
could just as easily show how a life

resembles a forest   a telephone
a symphony   a rainy day in Greece

114

or I could have said "imagine these lives
the man's and the city's   as two trains
speeding down parallel tracks while people
lean dangerously out of the windows
trying to clasp hands or pass messages
to each other"   or "suppose these lives

were visitors walking down a long dim
hallway in an ancient castle who must
keep lighting torches to show the way but
in that light they see   all along their course
relics of the past   some lovely and some
terrifying   which make them pause—they might
not make it to the end—but without the
torches their path is much too dark to see"

III. The Sandwich as Symbol

of course there are no ancient castles in
Clarksdale's vicinity   and weeds poke up
through the old railroad tracks   but that's the point
about metaphor   it's not limited

to reality   whereas history
is harder to mess with (though many have
succeeded): you're stuck with what's already
there   but that includes—if you pay attention—

plenty of symbols   which as I've said can
in their own way shape and clarify   as
this actual sandwich does for Aaron
Henry's story and for Clarksdale's   the place:

another Democratic Convention
Chicago   1968 when young
radicals fill the streets   angry this time
less about civil rights than the war in

Vietnam   Hubert Humphrey must wrestle
the nomination away from Eugene
McCarthy   while Mayor Richard Daley
famously proclaims "the police are not

in the streets to create disorder, they
are in the streets to preserve disorder"
Aaron Henry attends this convention
too but the situation is much changed:

in the wake of the national party's
1964 embarrassment (on
top of everything else the official
Mississippi "regular" Democrats

came out for the Republican ticket)
a group of white and black liberals has
outmaneuvered the old guard to become
the state's delegation to Chicago
chaired by Aaron Henry   the sandwich in
question appears at a meeting between
this delegation and Hubert Humphrey
who has a special rapport with Henry—

they're both pharmacists as well as allies
in politics—Humphrey asks some members
to chat with him and Orville Freeman   an
old friend and strategist in his campaign
(and Secretary of Agriculture)
Henry and the others are kept standing
in the hotel corridor for about
an hour   some barely persuaded to wait

this was   to use a sports analogy
"strike one"   finally admitted they sit
down at a huge round table and wait just
a bit more for their hosts   next they are told
by Humphrey that he wants them to simply

turn over some of their delegation's
seats representing Mississippi to
the un-credentialed (and discredited)

"regulars" they have just defeated in
federal court to get to Chicago
("I still wonder" says an eyewitness "what
on earth the party was thinking")   and an
evidently oblivious Humphrey
seems puzzled at the lack of response as shock
mounts to anger and Henry tries "to keep
the conversation going in his best

statesman-like manner"   by now it's early
afternoon   of course no one has had lunch:
the door opens on a waiter bearing
a big tray—which does immediately
improve the general mood   he proceeds
to set two large sandwiches on the table
in front of Humphrey and Freeman and then
departs   they begin eating   Humphrey keeps

talking   "in a room full of Southerners"
says the informant   "forget the color
line   nothing could be more discourteous"
at which point Aaron Henry seated next
to Humphrey sees "in a panic" that his
members have had enough and are ready
to stand up and leave   so in the words of
this participant in the meeting (as

reported in the book about Henry)
he "reached over while talking spiritedly
to Hubert...took a section of sandwich
and began to eat it. Hubert looked as
though he'd been pole axed. Aaron continued
to chat, leaning in at Hubert, nibbling

away. Ah, it was just a wonderful
moment. All of the Southerners relaxed

even smiled faintly—trying to stay
polite.... Aaron...ate about half the sandwich
in the most natural kind of way—a
moment of grace indeed! He finished up...
we...said our warm farewells and went home with
all the seats we'd come with"   really what makes
the sandwich symbolic of course is his
gesture   in the presence of power he

appropriates a piece—not all—of what
should be shared   seizing it in a way that
is a shock to authority   but can
not be taken as an offense because
the conversation never ceases: in
Aaron Henry's life and Clarksdale's life it
is this gesture that I cling to for my
own sense of meaning and understanding

The Lesson for Me

on my visits to Clarksdale—where I seem
to myself such an ignorant stranger—
both metaphor and symbol guide me at
times: the substance of history seen or

unseen   messy or neatly in place   lies
under the present   and must be acknowledged
as part of it   and I realized that
one way of looking at my own life is:

before and after Clarksdale   meaning that
only when I started visiting there—
shopping   talking to people   reading the
newspaper—did it occur to me that

the segregated North   where I live   is
Jim Crow not by law but by a feeling
of distance not possible in Clarksdale
where a basic fact of living is the

inescapable presence of everyone
which is one of the gifts from Clarksdale to
me that keeps me going back   this being
the kind of gift that's useful because I

have nothing else like it   and useful too
for the way it makes clear how vital to
Clarksdale the other sandwich is: the actual
shared sandwich   I see the city itself

at its best asking to be taken as
Aaron Henry's gesture writ large—symbols
do that: concrete object and act diffuse
meaning outward   if it was Henry whose

spirit revealed to him that the sandwich
and the conversation were equally
crucial   it occurs to me that what I
honor most in Clarksdale is the extent

to which this revelation suffuses
the place   it is a constant presence: the
sandwich generously or grudgingly
shared   offered gracefully or snatched up   and

the conversation   peaceful   hostile or
humorous   deeply felt   casual   calm
or too tense to be carried on without
interruption   bitter at City Hall

meetings   shouted in the pages of the
Clarksdale Press Register or on the street
the conversation over lunch between
bursts of laughter or whispered or wept at—

secret or public   heavy or light
this conversation that Aaron Henry
helped open up   that he would not shrink from
or refuse   that I have learned to respect

as an act of courage   and to embrace
as a symbol of the Clarksdale I love:
this conversation never ceases

Dear Manager

after lunch with Andy Carr at the Rest
Haven my wife and I joke that there are
some topics we must manage to avoid
discussing with Andy   his politics
being conservative and quite far from
our left end of the spectrum   but then it
occurs to me that (as so often in
Clarksdale) the joke is on me   since it was

Andy and his brother Oscar   third
generation cotton planters   who were
telling their peers in 1965
that the condition of poor people in
Mississippi and the Delta must be
addressed   while in the comfort of New York
bohemia I was hanging out in
the East Village honing my poems and

reading the news about Mississippi
with the righteous anger of an ardent
observer   so I have sense enough now
to regard Andy with wonder and
awe: after coming home from the navy
he had spent ten years settling down to life
as one of Clarksdale's solid citizens
and then more or less suddenly he was

chairman of the county's community
action agency—a biracial group
getting federal grants to run the new
antipoverty programs   and in the
newspaper instead of being quoted
about the Cotton Producers Institute
now he was describing the condition of
thousands in Coahoma County afflicted

by "unemployment   dilapidated
housing   poor health   hopelessness   when incomes
in this nation are at an all-time high and
the products of abundance are everywhere"
and Andy himself sought the help of the
Farmers Home Administration to build new
houses for his farm laborers — first time
for this kind of loan in Mississippi—

among Andy and Oscar's colleagues in
the Clarksdale farmer community
and most of the civic leadership   these
enterprises were less than popular
suspected as they were of being an
extension of the civil rights movement
and though not explicitly political
the various neighborhood centers did

focus on getting the poor (most of them
black) motivated and involved   or as
Andy points out with impeccable logic
"when you get people together   you are
going to talk about your needs and that's
politics"   what   I ask him   did he say
to his white planter friends about this kind
of attempt to—in effect—undo the

very order they lived by: the present
situation (he told them practically)
wasn't going to last   also he saw
what he was doing not as "liberal
versus conservative" but a "moral
cause"   now I'm trying to envision life
not in my 1965 East Village
but in 1965 Mississippi

where civil rights activism might be
met with beatings and killings   and here is
Andy   unfortified by any young

activist peers—no longer young nor by
habit an activist   sticking his neck
out   as he puts it to me   joining the
NAACP   (unkindest cut of
all no doubt)   with black people in his house

as guests   and one memorable day "we
had an integrated dinner at high
noon in a crowded Holiday Inn where
everybody ate   a whole bunch of blacks
and whites waited for a table to be
cleared   these things" he says "were absolutely
forbidden in my culture   we made quite
a splash"   and he laughs now about the fact

that in his church—Saint Elizabeth's—most
of the members are Italian (and were
thus barred from the country club almost as long
as the Jews) "people see me coming they
not only see civil rights or Negro-
lover but Roman Catholic"   I'm amused
and astonished by the mix of rebel
and scamp and patrician planter—and his

cool nerve—I'm also mystified by this
Annapolis graduate   scoutmaster
director of the First National Bank
vice president of the Delta Council
(a proud bastion of the established
order) the group "through which professional
agricultural and business leaders"
in the Delta work "together to solve

problems and promote the development"
of the economy   I wonder how
deep inside himself did this man seek and
delve for the unbending iron will to
insist that it must all change—sure he felt
it was a "moral cause"   so did I   but

that abstraction will take you exactly
as far as I got: the East Village

pondering moral causes from a wise
distance   no   the abstract must be made flesh
in the concrete: just inserting the word
"beauty" in a poem does not make the
poem beautiful   what does that is the
power of some concrete image   having
an idea   even a belief   will
not move you into action unless it

finds embodiment: I think back through my
talks with Andy   curious about what
it was that got transubstantiated
someplace in his life: once he told me that
for more than ten years of his growing up
a nurse lived with his family starting
when Andy was nine   someone he always
liked   admired   "a rather educated

very Christian black nurse" says Andy "one
of the greatest Christian influences
in my life   when I got to be twelve (that's
the age when they start calling you mister)
I wanted her to call me something else
so she said 'well I'll call you *manager*'"
and off to the navy at eighteen he's
in boot camp and "miserable early

on as a sailor" and "she would write me
'Dear Manager   remember   manager
the darkest hour is just before dawn   read
Matthew such and such a verse'   and I just
think I have a little more regard for
people not being treated rightly"   and
I imagine a ship   young Andy first
time far from home   in the closing days of

World War II   ahead of him the Naval
Academy   ten years in the service
then home to farming   business   marriage and
family   in short: life in Clarksdale which
could turn out quiet and comfortable—
does he have any inkling   young Andy
that he'll also become one of the more
unlikely revolutionaries in

the Delta?   I don't know   all I am shown
in my imagining is Andy   the
ship   the night sky maybe as dark as the
Delta sky   the stars as bright   but the rest
strange   not vast cotton but vast water
perhaps he has just closed his Bible and
come on deck after reading a letter
to "Dear Manager"   perhaps he looks out

over the vastness of the sea   sixty
years later we talk in his living room
his wife Susie serves iced tea   and I've brought
doughnuts   well he'll have one as he says "for
fellowship"   and later after a long
conversation he wants to know "How are
you going to write poetry about
all this?"   no no dear manager   I'm just

recording it   you have made the poem
yourself   and what was that verse from Matthew
anyway?   maybe where Jesus blesses
the poor then the meek then those "who hunger
and thirst for righteousness" or   as you stood
watch in the dark further from land than you
had ever been   maybe it was more concrete
and closer to home   where Jesus says

"he that hath received seed into the good ground
is he that heareth the word, and understandeth"

The Camel Chronicles, Continued

Act V: Chafik Shows Up, a Mississippi Political Mystery Is Solved, And a Date for the Race Is Set

the Online Register *itself seems to*
have disappeared from November 5th till
right after Christmas   and the Preacher too
has "withdrawn from the limelight"   all caused by
some "powerful figures of Italian
descent in Atlantic City" (Mafia
joke) who are distressed by the Register's
reporting on the "camel connection"

the problem is fixed with a few phone calls
to a group called "My friends in Buffalo"
so the tale resumes: Chafik has returned
as suddenly as he vanished   he's found
one morning after being gone eight
days "in his familiar seat at the back
table"   but unwilling to speak   nervous
obviously traumatized by something—

"threadbare tweed sport jacket   conspicuous
bulge over his left hip" like an old film
noir hero   and reaching instinctively
for it every time the front door opens—
Chafik's absence had coincided with
Mississippi's election season: a
lively one this year partly because of
Governor Fordice's predicament

nearly killed election night when his car
crashed   he was on the way home from Memphis

where he had been seen dining with—as it
is sometimes phrased—a woman not his wife
"pro-family values Republican"
is how one article describes him and
he's still recuperating   not speaking
publicly   it's not known what caused the crash

but the Online Register's *got the jump*
on mainstream media: check the Memphis
Commercial Appeal *or the* LA Times   *you won't*
find out that "witnesses claim they saw what
appeared to be a crazy man in an
unraveling turban racing across
the interstate on a two-humped camel,
screaming for his life"   since neither Fordice

nor Chafik is talking we are left as
the Register *puts it with unanswered*
questions about: doctored polls (the horse won
but no one will admit voting that way)
organized crime   legalization of
camel racing in Mississippi and
Chafik's connection to the governor
but it's time to get back to the great race

the event seems to be drawing closer
as Jimmy Walker appoints himself chair
(and only member) of the "Camel/Horse
Racing Committee" and declares a date:
next summer during Clarksdale's big Delta
Jubilee   perhaps with some backing from
the casinos who just might be willing
to set odds and handle the betting

                    * * *

another step up for Clarksdale   which now
in the person of Chafik emerges

as the force behind Mississippi's most
sensational political scandal

and since the casinos—which till now have
been referred to only casually—
are easing into place as potential
players (no doubt there's money to be made)

here's a note: the "gaming industry" boom
in Mississippi dates from the state law
(1990) that permits "cruise vessels"
in state waters to host these casinos

"built on floating barges before being
fixed to the shoreline" one article says
so down through the north Delta and at the
Gulf Coast thirty-one such palaces

attract customers   increase the tax base:
good news for Tunica County—closest
to Memphis—which has nine   nearly a third
of the total   in Coahoma County

there's just one: thirty minutes from Clarksdale
right where the bridge crosses to Helena
Arkansas (if I may quote a proverb
myself "location location location")

this was once the "Lady Luck Casino"
twin palaces side by side: one with a
huge neon saxophone in front   its
theme being "rhythm and blues"   the other

with a neon cowboy hat just as big
indicating the "country" theme—this
used to be called "separate but equal":
"self-segregation" is a newer term

but recently "Lady Luck" has become
an "Isle of Capri"—a chain of fourteen
casinos in the South and Midwest—with
a single corporate "tropical" theme

(that squawk you hear is live parrots) so is
this "good news"   "bad news"   or "no opinion"?
and you may vote here on the whole question
of Mississippi casino gambling

("yes" "no" or "unsure")   the article—called
"Vegas on the Delta"—can be found   where
else   on the Internet   but it does not
discuss the prospects for camel racing

Act VI: Finale: Chafik Returns to Normal, the Horse Forces Are Ready, the Confederacy Seeks a Camel (and a Camel Jockey) But, Despite Many Developments, the Race Has Yet to Transpire

it's New Year's Day when Chafik Chamoun as
if waking from a trance snaps back into
life   exchanging insults with friends "you dumb
Ay-rab"   "you dumb redneck" etcetera
meanwhile a "Horseman's Guild" of supporters
(presumably the Preacher and others)
has secured the services of Carol
Kozlowsky the professional rider

from New York and one champion
horse while the "Camel Confederacy"
(Chafik   Grady Palmer   Jimmy Walker)
is still casting about for an entry
so Chafik   now fully recovered   heads
for the United Arab Emirates
to meet the president   a booster of
camel racing   maybe he'll donate one

impressed with Dubai's camel breeding and
training facilities Chafik faxes
blueprints home: Jimmy Walker enlists James
Butler (Clarksdale Public Works Director)
who believes a "modest camel stable"
could be built next to the Clarksdale Country
Club if disguised as "routine drainage work"
but then the Dubai connection falls through

so Chafik looks to the underground black
market Eastern Europe camel racing
circuit   quickly dispatching agents to
Romania: his daughter   her husband
who return shortly with an "adopted
child" alleged by the Register *to be*
not a child at all but a ringer: an
ace thirty-five-year-old "camel jockey"

in other news Grady Palmer retains
his seat as City Commissioner and
Ambassador to Norway after he
unveils plans for a huge camel racing
coliseum in Clarksdale   the newly
elected Mayor is described as a longtime
Camel Confederacy supporter
and by now we are almost in July

the Jubilee has come and gone without
the promised encounter   although as a
good faith gesture Jimmy Walker and his
wife did show up there on a camel   but
something scared the beast and off it went down
the road at a great clip with Jimmy and
Helen still aboard   perhaps an omen
that plans for the Great Race remain troubled

❉

When He Wakes

Genesis: Introduction to a Song Written By Vasti Jackson and Performed By Koko Taylor

on the first day Mother Blues rolled back the
big waters to reveal the Delta   on
the second she planted cottonwood   ash
hickory   tupelo   walnut   cypress
on the third day red panther   bear   squirrel
mosquitoes   on the fourth she sighed and sang—
out came Mound Builders   Choctaw   Chickasaw
 "humans" she thought "may complicate my life"

and some of them did   DeSoto   the French
and British   the state of Mississippi
on the fifth day someone brought in the slaves
Mother Blues feared she was losing control
on the sixth day when the Choctaw left their
homes forever she sang the "Treaty of
Dancing Rabbit Creek Blues" quickly followed
by her "Bound and Whipped in the Cotton Field Blues"

Mother Blues was tired and knew she would need
that seventh day to rest but first she sought
the cruelest cotton planter   cleared a
space at the edge of his land and built a
cabin   invited the weariest field
hands and the ones who had been secretly
learning her craft   and it was Saturday
night and she said "now let the juke joint jump"

Mother and Son

"Now, Mr. Fred, you come in here tomorrow night,
don't bring me none of that Dizzy Gillespie music."
—Howlin' Wolf to Fred Robinson (Abu Talib), from an
interview with Abu Talib, *Living Blues* 144

1

Blues   mother of Jazz   wishes to locate
her son   who sometimes wanders off   gets lost

his mama loves him of course   even when
he forgets where he's from   with his smart mouth

if you know where he is please ask him to
get back in touch   Mother Blues misses him

2

"Jazz is a good boy" she says   "till he gets
mixed up with some lowlife crowd in nice suits…"

Mother Blues admits to being old-school
spends her life dressed in those same damn three chords

"well" she says "once in awhile maybe four
but if chords were nickels that boy would be rich"

3

"what's music" Mother Blues has always said
"unless someone sings and the people dance"

when her son Jazz comes to visit she suspects that
he's embarrassed by such carryings-on

"no, Mother" he says "I am proud of you
but my music is very serious"

134

4

Mother Blues respects his sophistication
but she still wishes he'd never left home:

she remembers how when Jazz was little
he'd sit on her lap while she sang to him—

back then she taught him all of her old songs
and now Jazz hears them faintly in his sleep sometimes:
when he wakes they're gone and he misses his mama

Clarksdale Blues

"I like these" says Bob   a Brooklyn comment
on my Clarksdale poems   "now I want to
hear about musicians today   the ones
who came along after Robert Johnson"

here they are Bob: I haven't met them all
(twice a year visitor that I am) but
these are the ones who came after him—though
some not by much—and I'll tell you that in

this town—like nowhere else I've been at least—
that tradition is not just unbroken
but getting passed on   Johnson and Son House
Pinetop Perkins   Robert Junior Lockwood

were part of it   Muddy   Wolf   Sonny Boy
and Robert Nighthawk   whose son Sam Carr you
might find in Clarksdale   as we did one night
at Red's juke joint   his touch on that snare still

so soft and sure (though Sam was then in his
seventies) that playing sax with him as
drummer I felt I was in a small tight
boat lifted by waves and not coming down

* * *

Sam and many others played in Little
Jeno Tucker's "All-Stars"   Jeno's smile was
anxious and welcoming at the same time
and I thought him the sweetest soul in town

when I find Big Jack in Clarksdale he might
be in his kitchen getting a haircut

136

or just back from fishing or down at Red's
with a Coke in the cool afternoon dark

if you see Super Chikan on stage but
(still thinking he's some kind of quaint rustic)
you don't understand the intelligence
watch the eyes   you'll find he's laughing at you

Sunday night heading straight from the airport
to Red's   I find "Big T" Terry Williams
in mid-guitar-solo—no time to talk
but he flashes me something like "Welcome"

* * *

Wade Walton played guitar   harp   recorded
a now rare album   cut hair in his own
barber shop   could lay down rhythm with a
razor strop and—some say—dance at the same time

he played with Big Jack   and Clarksdale's other
favorite sons   John Lee Hooker   Muddy
Waters   Ike Turner   when he died the town
honored him   no room here to quote it all

just this praise from the Sunflower River
Blues Association chairman: "he was with
blues a long time" said Melville Tillis "and
he gave me my first haircut on credit...."

* * *

at Sarah's Kitchen and Blues Café here's
CV Veal   old enough to have performed
with Ike Turner (which he did—wearing this
same baseball hat?)   when he sings   a force—not

just in his voice but surrounding his body—
hurls me across the stage (some electric charge?)
if they did sing together he
must have blown poor Ike right out of the room

* * *

"hey Sax Man!"   Wesley "Junebug" Jefferson
yells across the parking lot   asks me to
sit in tonight—he knows that's exactly
what I just came 1400 miles to do

* * *

the first musician I met was "Doctor
Mike" James performing with his young students
"they call him Doctor" the old line goes "'cause
he makes you feel so good"—one of those kids

was Venessia Young   in college now:
she nods to me on her way to the stage
with her "Pure Blues Express"   self-possessed   quiet
but when she grabs a guitar it's time

to run for cover   and Jacqueline: nine
years old with a wiry intense Gypsy
look when I saw her in Mike's class   next thing
I know she's thirteen   flying to LA

(with her mother) where big shots are showing
interest   local musicians are hoping
that she succeeds   and that as the proverb
says   you can't take Clarksdale out of the girl

* * *

Mister Johnny Billington—that master
teacher—leads the Midnighters—a band of

his young students   each year some move on and
new ones move in   it was Mister Johnny's

vision   before anyone else   that you
could teach kids to play the blues   on my first
visit Fred Hicks   Lee Williams   Anthony
Sherrod (sax/drums/bass) were the Midnighters

thirteen years old when we sat them down to
record for my CD: the session ran long
I forgot teenagers must eat   Jack and
Jeno left   came back with buckets of fried chicken

two years later Fred was a singer   Lee
and Anthony were playing with Jeno's
son Artrell in Jeno's last band: Lee still
on drums   Anthony now as lead guitar

that year Jack was not at the festival:
I worried I wouldn't get to play but
Jeno was generous "can you give me
some help" he said and there I was on stage

Jack and Jeno grew up together   the
Press Register said Jeno was sitting
in his car when he had the heart attack
died   at age 59   the sweetest soul

* * *

I like to jam with the Deep Cuts—Doctor
Mike   Josh Stewart   plus my old friends Lee and
Anthony   this band has T-shirts and sharp
stage names: "Butcher Knife" "Razorblade" "Switchblade"

"Pocket Knife" (for Lee   who's "in the pocket"
as good drummers are said to be) one night
at Sarah's when they invite me up they
insist I need a nickname too   I am

embarrassed: middle-aged middle-class guy
from up north just trying to fit into
a Clarksdale blues band without being too
noticeable "OK   call me Nail File"

* * *

more than ten years now I've been visiting:
long enough to witness how tradition
remains   grows   shifts direction   grows   withers
grows again   always the blues   and so

the demise of these blues in the Delta—
reported now and then with ironic
relish by journalists dropping in for
a brief tour—is like Mark Twain's joke about

the news of his death having been greatly
exaggerated: evidently they
didn't stay long enough for a Thursday night
at Sarah's when sly Mister Johnny (in

suit and tie) might turn up to check out the
young players   the Deep Cuts play a set first
maybe with some guests   and then the students—
last time I was there a child just turned six

set loose by his mother wandered toward
the stage   climbed up behind the drum set   he
already has his musician's nickname
they call him "Big Man"   starts playing behind

some teenagers and astonishingly
he locks in the beat   he's a real drummer
not yet floating like Sam   not as deep
in the pocket as Lee   but he will be

listening to them I recognize the song now:
they're playing "The Thrill Is Gone"   but it isn't

Twelve Blues Bars

Adam and Eve's Blues Bar was forced out of
business but the memory has stayed with us

opening night at the Cottonfield Blues Bar:
no shortage of well-rehearsed performers

at the Underground Railroad Blues Bar all
the harp players understood train whistles

Ma Rainey's voice came blasting out of the
Big Tent Blues Bar to kick Jim Crow's sorry ass

When Robert Johnson's broom needed dusting
he'd head for the Crossroads Lounge in Clarksdale

cops on the trail of the People's Blues Bar
heard faint music but never found the source

in search of that blues bar look   the nightclub
owner dressed Leadbelly in overalls

one Texas or Chicago night some fool
plugged all the guitars into amplifiers

getting ready to sit down at lunch counters
they sing all night at the Freedom Blues Bar

quaint folk art on the walls at the new House
of Blues but no photos of the lynchings

Heaven is a blues bar: the gates of Hell
are inscribed "Welcome to the Airport Lounge"

ghost train pulls up at the Depot Blues Bar
Muddy steps out and says "it's good to be home"

Lives of the Bluesmen

one of my favorite Clarksdale bluesmen
took me to church with him where he is a
respected member   plays guitar backing
the choir   thus it's clear that—for some at least—
the old feud has eased up: blues is no
longer always seen as "music of the
devil"   in fact from my reading lately
I've been struck rather by the parallels

between church teachings and blues   thus in *Lives
of the Saints* an archbishop's foreword speaks
of "faith" "religion" "saints"   but you could just
as easily   I thought   substitute "blues"
or "bluesmen" (and women) in the same places:
"We live in a sophisticated, if
not cynical age in which the former
'certainties' of *blues*, which brought comfort to

so many, are now widely questioned. But
surely a living *blues* can have no absolute
certainties?" and (in my version) he goes
on: "*Blues* by very definition, grows
through a constant, indeed daily, process,
whereby doubts, old and new, must ever be
conquered afresh"   well   isn't this just how
the blues lives in us? and further:

"This growth in *blues* can be helped by stories
and legends of the *bluesmen*...heroic
men and women" he says (in my mind now
he's become the Archbishop of Blues) who
"have bequeathed to us an inspiration
that transcends ordinary history"
how acute this archbishop: stories and
legends   passing down the generations

of Delta blues: the bluesman clowning at
John Lee Hooker's club doing the "white folks'
yodel"   then his own version of Hooker
himself who comes up on stage   "I'm gonna
show you how to do it son"   and when they
talk later "your grandpa named Ellis Johnson?
lived down around by Rena Lara?   I
know your grandpa   hell he was the best damn

fiddle player in the South"   "so that *was*
y'all I saw when I was a kid" says the
younger bluesman   then Hooker recalls
that there was always "a bunch of
little brats around the house" "I would
always be the one" says the bluesman
"sittin' right there by him"   "little bitty
red one" says John Lee Hooker   "yeah that was

me"   "oh" says Hooker   "I remember"
and there are the miracles: the bluesman
who traveled wherever he wanted by
Greyhound bus   strolling out to the highway
he would just stand a certain way as the
bus approached   a secret Masonic sign:
the driver (like him they were all Masons) would
screech to a stop so he could get on   and

the bluesman whose voice at eighty might crack
glass   shaking the roof one night at Red's so
that it leaked even harder   and of course
the countless cures   the lame and the halt up
dancing—my archbishop was right: your doubts
old and new through that constant that daily
process are conquered afresh in Clarksdale
you hear stories and legends   you transcend

ordinary history   if only
the archbishop himself was here I would

congratulate him on his insight   and
try to help rescue him from the present
cynical age so he could be restored
to his comfort and joy in the living blues

The Camel Chronicles Concluded

Rhetorical Afterthoughts in Two Parts

1. A Pleasant Lunch and an Unpleasant Surprise

non-sentimentalists (in Meredith's
terms) willing to incur further debt as
the price of enjoyment should find
both as we amble toward conclusion—

for readers who are sentimentalists
this is a good place to stop: if you have
been entertained thus far I'll acknowledge
that this is the point where we start to lose

focus on the camel/horse argument
which reverts to more insults and private
jokes—an unkind critic might recall the
old TS Eliot canard about

ending not with a bang etcetera—
the jokes are less funny   the debt mounts up
but to those who hang on I'll say I don't
think of the *Chronicles* as just winking

out with no big climax but rather as
swirling up out of Clarksdale into
communion with the world even though the
final installment can't give more than a

vague promise that "all questions…will one day
be answered" and as I came to those last
words   one phrase—"camel jockey"—from somewhere
in those final few episodes   had a

familiar ring though I couldn't place it
and right then I went off to Clarksdale   so
I put it aside—this time with Robert's
help I found the Preacher   but by now my

poem was almost finished   so this was
not like being in the middle of a
novel but as if you had read to the
end and now you got to meet one of the

characters   who could tell you whether the
author had represented them fairly
and what had gone on happening after
you closed the book   we had lunch at—where else?

the Preacher was now seven years older
(like all of us) than when the *Chronicles*
had begun unfolding   he graciously
cleared up a few items that I had been

wondering about   (first assuring me
that the tale is indeed not over yet)
in real life he doesn't thunder about
false prophets but gives cool explanations:

Chafik's "disappearance"?—some surgery
which   when bandaged up   did resemble the
film noir pistol—and the Preacher says his own
family has been associated

with horses and riding for years—hence his
passion on that subject is factual
and Ms. Kozlowsky he says is a real
trainer—and in on the joke   then he says—

is he pulling my leg?—he's recently
heard from a few interested parties
who might want to sponsor the race along
the course envisioned from here to Memphis

the Preacher likes the prospect of bettors
and spectators lining the highway up
around the Tunica casinos   sees
promise of big revenue for Clarksdale

(and lest you think that I'm pulling *your* leg
I refer you to Clarksdale's other news
source   the *Press Register*   which reports   some
years later now   on a competing

possibility: a big racetrack in
Tunica—construction not yet finally
approved—which could unhappily hijack
such a huge event and all its profits)

so the Preacher hopes (along with many
more of us I'm sure   if not really the
Pontifical Academy   though who knows)
to find out someday if the camel or

the horse is faster   and by the way
he tells me   even the Romanian
adopted child is real   which brings back
that nagging thought about "camel jockeys"

home from Clarksdale I checked the Internet
which only took about five seconds to
remind me: "trafficking of child camel
jockeys to United Arab Emirates"

in other words—terrific irony—
here we are with slavery again   the
UN getting reports every year now
of children as young as three or four sold

or kidnapped from Pakistan   India
Bangladesh   beaten   semi-starved for speed
and lightness   mounted on camels   perhaps
the very one that began the quarrel

it doesn't seem fair to find slavery
behind every innocent camel joke
but there's my point—the tree falling   a thing
done   you hear it   you read it   you own it

2. *In Which It Is Shown That Poets Are Ace Non-Sentimentalists*

what I mean is that our job skills include
the ability to let one person
event   object   remind us of many
others   so if George Meredith had wished
to find someone for whom a "thing done" could
never be detached from any of its
consequences   the most obvious or
the most remote   someone who hears the tree

fall and knows that "attention must be paid"—
if he needed someone who displayed these
qualifications he would have placed an
ad for a poet   of course this talent
doesn't appeal to everyone—people
don't like to walk around all day getting
reminded of things   which is why the most
important poets are not   as they say

household words   like William Carlos Williams
who bequeathed us along with his poems
a simple proverb: "no ideas but
in things"   turn that a bit inside out and
you have "all things suggest ideas":   to
apply this—in our case—you look at the
Parthenon and reflect how its beauty
is inextricable from slave labor

or at dusk over the Mississippi
out behind one of the great casinos
your mind lights on "tax base" "wealth" or "pawn shop"

and if you see a Confederate flag
in Clarksdale the thought this flag suggests will
depend on your personal history
your politics   your ethnicity and
possibly what you learned from your parents

and if we add juxtaposition   place
things side by side to see if they connect—
set the flag/casino/Parthenon next
to Chafik's stuffed camel   Grady Palmer's
third cup of coffee   a Bible   a sack
of cotton   the restored house of John Clark
the founder   the saw of Thamneus   the
cabin where Muddy Waters lived   or those

railroad tracks that lead out of town and also
divide it—sure enough   with my job skills
I can do all that   but then there's no way
to tell what *you* will be reminded of
as I recount these *Camel Chronicles*:
all the stuff I've thrown in here just banging
around for readers to grab if they can—
how do I know what it will suggest to

you or what you'll accuse me of   making
jokes about religion?   taking solid
citizens too lightly   or too seriously?
insensitivity to—you name it:
in response I first invoke the Williams
defense as laid out above   then present
with a brief comment the apocryphal
(I think) story of Michelangelo

and his frustrated apprentice   "Master
I have been with you ten years and still can't
figure out how to carve a block of stone
into the shape of a horse"   "my young friend"
the great sculptor replies "you simply take
your tools and cut away everything that

does not resemble the horse" (or camel
presumably)   the point is that to write

the poem you don't need to make something
that was never there till now but only
to shape what you find yourself in front of
to let it start reminding you of things
which it will: because we can't extricate
ourselves from the world   in other words   we
are all embedded in history   or
again   once we understand how Clarksdale

seeks   declares its connection with the world
even becoming a player on what is
famously called the "world stage"   then we can't
escape anything we say being used
if not as evidence against us   at
least as proof that our stories cannot be
purified of this human connection
that—as Lear said—"smells of mortality"

or on the other hand Walt Whitman   more
sanguine than Lear on the same subject:
"I celebrate myself, I sing myself"
and "I am large, I contain multitudes"

My Conclusion

and thus does Clarksdale contain multitudes:
from Robert Johnson to the Pope   from King
Cotton to Jim Crow to the Rest Haven
where anyone can come in for breakfast

from Michelangelo admiring the
lifelike figure of Muddy Waters at
the museum to Williams who insists
in my ear that what is real and what is

revelatory about Clarksdale are
the same   from Shakespeare (you know he's here because
so many blues songs scan just like blank verse)
to the old porches where we drink sweet tea

from the 1850s Know Nothings in
the Delta trying to keep out all the
Catholics and foreigners to Chafik
and Louise here 50 years and counting

("We didn't come on no Queen Mary" says
Chafik)   from innocent camel racing
jokes to the news (and all its echoes) that
slavery did not die with the Old South

and isn't this an assortment   you and
me and these multitudes here in Clarksdale
(which is to say the world) where George Meredith's
tree falls   first in the forest that will yield

to cotton fields   then in the desert
in the form of a camel crushing some
six-year-old jockey caught beneath its feet
which only proves that those of us who choose

to be non-sentimentalists can grab
our share of the debt anywhere any
time   but remember—very important—
that though we remain willing to incur

this debtorship for things done   we are not
proscribed from enjoying   rather—on the
contrary—our enjoyment runs deeper
than that of the sentimentalists just

because we have made the choice to take on
the burden—and the fact that I've chosen
Clarksdale for joy and debtorship both is
no doubt the source of the obsession I

have already mentioned   so in August
I joke to friends "I've got to get away
from this New England heat"   then I fly to
Memphis   rent a car   and I can't express

how happy   purely happy I am to
be on my way   down 61: fast food/
casinos/cotton fields   and then Clarksdale!
left on Second to Up-Town Motor Inn

which is right downtown   are there any jam
sessions tonight?   who should I phone first?   is
the Blues Museum open?   and when I get
home my mind is often still in Clarksdale

taking a slow walk through the center of
town   crossing the oldest streets   savoring
those names: "SUNFLOWER" (next to the river)
"DELTA"   "YAZOO" (for that other river

an old word of disputed origin:
maybe Choctaw for "hunting ground" or for
"mud with a bad smell" or "river of death"
or—as a sax player—my favorite

"to blow on an instrument"   though this one
is from a list made in 1902)
"ISSAQUENA" (perhaps from "issa"/deer
and "okhina"/river)   here the "New World"

district—black music   shops   Saturday nights
when everyone mixed together—flourished
till maybe the 1950s   not much
left now   "LEFLORE" (first name Greenwood   half Choctaw

half French planter who prospered after the
treaty of Dancing Rabbit Creek in the
1830s)   "SHARKEY" (Judge William L
briefly governor of Mississippi

appointed 1865 after
the Civil War by President Johnson—
interesting to speculate how   when
why this street got its name—) and finally

"DESOTO"   that Spanish explorer (what
does "discover" mean?   did I "discover"
Clarksdale?) who first viewed the Mississippi
probably from somewhere near here   (and one

of history's great sentimentalists
he was too   enjoying power without
much regard for the Choctaw or other
recipients of his massacres   and

wouldn't he have felt right at home here   three
hundred years on   as a slave-owning
cotton planter   or later   weeping over
Birth of a Nation   but as it was he

died—body thrown into the great river
thus   sadly   DeSoto never got to
enjoy the New World district or face an
international war crimes tribunal)

but again I digress   what I meant to
say was (and I don't defend this narrow-
mindedness   but there it is) that—while I
acknowledge the Peabody-to-Vicksburg

claim and the hard facts on the road map—the
Delta that's been imprinted on me is
bounded by Clarksdale   which also (as I
hope I have shown) encompasses the world

and so   though I've seen a lot of places
(if not on DeSoto's scale)   and though I
love the Acropolis and hope to drink
wine again in the Plaka before I die

after that I want my ashes scattered
along that green stretch of park behind Red's
juke joint on the Sunflower's east bank which is
where my mind always starts out on these long slow walks

L'Envoi

Authentic

for Big Jack Johnson and Bob Bene

on stage with Big Jack: Bob the bass player
and I exchange glances   the eyes laughing
at insider jokes told by the music
like when Jack pounds a twelve-bar blues into
thirteen or fourteen or ten   later I
realize I'm laughing at myself—New
Jersey's answer to the Delta blues—for
my first reaction: *Big Jack played it wrong*

I imagine saying "Jack I know how
important this music is to you and all that—
growing up as you did playing the blues—
but I have to tell you: you got it wrong"

* * *

and so what makes it different when Jack
and I discuss history?   I've read books
about civil rights struggles   and been to
demonstrations   but Jack admonishes
"now   don't listen when someone tells you things
were bad"   and goes on to describe a kind
of Golden Age   where they had pigs   chickens
grew enough food for themselves and minded

their own business   you were sick they sent for
the doctor and you didn't have to pay
I think he's talking about sharecropping
his own growing up   the 40s   50s

* * *

should I say "Jack you've got it wrong again"?
should *I* tell *him* about the lynchings   the
indignities of those years   could it be
he's unaware of all the suffering
or does he have his own reasons for not
disclosing what I've only read about
for displaying a view of the past
that shocks me—and should I decide what's real?

no   I should just stick to my business on
stage   I will back you up Jack   I will swear
your testimony tonight is the truth
I'll swear you're telling it right   play the blues Jack

Whose Dark Night

far distant from Clarksdale Mississippi
a thousand miles from the Delta and back
in what some knew as the exuberant
1920s   F Scott Fitzgerald wrote
that "in the real dark night of the soul it is
always three o'clock in the morning"   far
removed as well from Saint John of the Cross
whose "dark night" was just the deep torturous

beginning of the journey towards God
while for Fitzgerald—though I'm guessing here—
I think "always" was the operative
word   and so the brief story I heard in
Clarksdale reminded me of Saint John but
also of Fitzgerald and I suppose
I'll never know which dark night this story
illustrates: a black woman friend told me

of her friend who was nursing an old white
lady   old enough that she must have been
around when Fitzgerald was writing   good
times for some in the Delta   was she well
off   maybe even a debutante?   or
just barely middle class?   in any case
there would have been black people—housekeeper
laundress   perhaps a nursemaid   cook   yard boy—

working for her family in those old
days when everything was so different
and now again   sick and old as she is
frail enough to need 24-hour care
she's got a black nurse at her side   and so
one night the old white lady wakes—in my
mind of course it's three o'clock—all alone
with the black woman in whose hands one could

say her life rests   she wakes and begins to
think of something—is it an incident
from her past? a wider reflection on
life in the Delta over many years?—
and in a voice I try to imagine
but can't—incredulous? tremulous? just
curious?—she asks her nurse "y'all didn't
mind that we beat y'all niggers' asses?"

and that's all   the story ends there leaving
me to guess her meaning   whose dark night she
was entering   Fitzgerald's or Saint John's: was
she saying "I accept my life as it is and
as it was" or "from this darkness I begin my journey"

The Hedgehog and the Fox

*The fox knows many things, but the hedgehog
knows one big thing*—Archilocus

for this mysterious fragment that got
me thinking about how I see Clarksdale
I have to thank the ancient Greek poet:
I recognized my one big thing   to dig
myself down into the earth of the blues
to write the book of blues rooted deep in
Clarksdale   dedicated and focused I
was the ancient Greek hedgehog of the blues

and reading the essay that parsed the old
riddle I reassured myself   finding
hedgehogs understood as those writers whose
"single universal organizing
principle"   whose "central vision" controls
and relates to everything else   after
awhile though   Clarksdale itself seemed to
be affecting my vision: my focus

rambled off through town like the fox   who in
the essay pursues many things that are
"scattered...diffused...unrelated...even
contradictory"—enchiladas for
lunch at Azimba with Maie and Yvonne
reminding me there's a new Mexican
community here   a day with English
classes at the high school immersing me

in tales of young Tom (not yet Tennessee)
Williams who spent the happy parts of his
childhood here   in his grandpa's Episcopal
rectory on Sharkey Street   history

draws me in   a great great great descendant
of planter/Governor Alcorn gives me
a wild tour of the family land from
fields to bayou to the governor's own

statue on its pedestal   Clarksdale's old
Lebanese neighborhood is gone but the
town remains anchored to the highway by
Lebanese restaurants (south by Chamoun's
palace of kibbie   north by the fragrance
of Abe's Barbecue) like a sturdy ship
in the Delta Sea   while my motel hosts
speak to each other in a language from

India   and there are more stories I
haven't told yet   but this fox is trotting
through one enormous meadow with no way
to tell them all   poets are fine but what
Clarksdale needs is its own classic novel:
it wouldn't be Austen I think but that
sly world-devouring fox Dickens who could
do Clarksdale as he did London: surely

he'd manage—like the great writers/foxes—
to "seiz[e] upon the essence of a vast
variety of experiences
and objects for what they are in themselves"
meanwhile once again it turns out the joke's
on me: after all my fooling around
with metaphor I had it just backwards:
it's Clarksdale digging so deep into me

it entangles my roots   and I cannot
go anywhere without Clarksdale panting
along beside me   if I'm reading a
Victorian novel   climbing the steps
of the Parthenon   when I lie down and
when I rise up   or sit in the dark to

contemplate my life   there's Clarksdale   and of
course on stage with a mouth full of sax and

a mind full of blues   the band in my head
is always complete: Fox on drums   Hedgehog
on bass   and with Clarksdale next to me on
vocals and guitar I feel like—as Muddy

Waters once put it—"I'm ready as anybody can be"

Notes on the Poems

In addition to specific citations, I am indebted overall to three important books: James C. Cobb's historical study, *The Most Southern Place on Earth*, Oxford University Press (1994); Constance Curry's biography of Aaron Henry, *The Fire Ever Burning*, University Press of Mississippi (2000); and Nicholas Lemann's study of Clarksdale, Chicago, and Washington's "War on Poverty," *The Promised Land: The Great Black Migration and How It Changed America*, Knopf (1991).

* * *

If the Delta Was the Sea
- "darkness upon…": Book of Genesis.
- "sea-change…": Shakespeare, *The Tempest*.

Rights
- Chickasaw Letters 1831: www.chickasawhistory.com/CHICL_31.htm.

The Camel Chronicles, Prologue:
- "Immense Debtorship," George Meredith, *The Ordeal of Richard Feverel*.
- Unless otherwise attributed, all quotes are from various episodes of the *Chronicles*: www.clarksdale.com/camel/.

So Italian
- Historical information primarily from Father Paul Canonici's book, *The Delta Italians*, Caló Creative Designs, Madison, Mississippi (2003).

The Wisdom of "Pap" Pang *or* Typecasting in the Delta
- "There never was a friend like Lee Gong": John Steinbeck, *Sweet Thursday*.
- "for business purposes…", "Growing up in Mississippi in the '40s–'60s": oral history, Bobby Joe Moon: usadeepsouth.com, http://usads.ms11.net/bjm.html.
- "everything within forty-nine square miles," "giving out silver dollars…": *The Most Southern Place on Earth*.

Pinteleh Yid
- The history of Clarksdale's Jewish community is drawn primarily from Margery Kerstine's extensively researched website: http://www.freewebs.com/deltahistory/. Abe Isaacson's unpublished manuscripts are in Clarksdale's Carnegie Public Library. The movie *Delta Jews* (1999) is by Mike DeWitt.

Aaron Henry's Sandwich
- "those small yellow buses…": *The Promised Land*. Other quotes and anecdotes in the poem come from Curry or Lemann; the sandwich story is from Curry; the "history text" is on file in the Carnegie Public Library.

The Camel Chronicles: Rhetorical Afterthoughts, Conclusion
- "attention must be paid": Arthur Miller, *Death of a Salesman*.
- trafficking of child camel jockeys: UN Commission on Human Rights, Sub-Commission on the Promotion and Protection of Human Rights, Working Group on Contemporary Forms of Slavery, 27th Session, Geneva, 27-31 May 2002: http://www.antislavery.org/archive/submission/submission2002-UAE.htm.
- "smells of mortality": Shakespeare, *King Lear*.
- "I celebrate myself…": Walt Whitman, *Song of Myself*.

Lives of the Bluesmen
- *Butler's Lives of the Saints: Concise Edition, Revised and Updated*, Alban Butler, Michael Walsh, foreword by Cardinal Basil Hume, Archbishop of Winchester, HarperCollins (1991).
- The John Lee Hooker and Greyhound anecdotes are based on conversations with James "Super Chikan" Johnson.
- The bluesman "whose voice…might crack glass" is Clarksdale's own C.V. Veal.

Whose Dark Night
- "in the real dark night of the soul," F. Scott Fitzgerald, *The Crack-Up*.
- I regret that it was necessary to directly quote a racially offensive term in this poem, in order to tell the story as I heard it, and to make the point about the persistence of racism.

The Hedgehog and the Fox
- Isaiah Berlin, *The Hedgehog and the Fox*, New York, Simon & Schuster (1953).

Special Thanks

Abby Freedman, my live-in editor, made this book possible through her wise suggestions and her constant encouragement.

Thanks as always to my Hanging Loose Press colleagues for their support, counsel, and generally uplifting spirit over the years I have worked at this project: Bob Hershon, Mark Pawlak, Donna Brook, and Marie Carter.

Thanks for skill, patience, and guidance to fellow writers Edward Hower, Richard Hoffman, Emmett Jarrett, Steve Seidel, and Adria Steinberg, whose advice took me through many drafts.

Thanks to proofreading genius Michael "Eagle Eye" LeBlanc.

* * * *

"The Camel Chronicles": This poem is dedicated with gratitude to protagonists Chafik Chamoun and Larry "The Preacher" Blades (who has confessed to authorship of the original episodes).

Annette Johnson has been a constant source of warmth and strength.

James "Super Chikan" Johnson has inspired me with his music and his conversation.

Panny Flautt Mayfield has shared her hospitality, her photographs, and her vast knowledge of Clarksdale and the blues.

Maie Smith welcomed me to the Delta Blues Museum and has offered more than ten years of her good cheer and steady friendship.

Yvonne Stanford has given generously of her advice, encouragement, and support for all my work in Clarksdale.

Terry "Big T" Williams has always made room for me to join him on stage for joyous blues music.

There is no place like Red's, and no better friend to musicians, to the blues, or to me than Red Paden.

"Dear Manager" hero Andrew Carr remains an inspiration.

* * * *

And I owe much gratitude to these Clarksdale and Delta friends who have shared their time with me through conversation and interviews, not only providing material for the poems, but also helping me sustain the will and the energy to write this book:

Rebecca Hood Adams, Mister Johnny Billington, Paul and Barbara Borgognoni, Roy and Rosalie Brown, Mara Califf, Louis Campassi, Paul Canonici, Sam Carr, Troy Catchings, Gilroy Chow, Don Clark, Laura "Lala" Craig, Missie Craig of Clarksdale's Carnegie Public Library, Sarah Crisler-Ruskey, the Delta Blues Museum staff, Toni Gooch, Benny Gooden, Eugene Gooden, Gary Halsey, Eugene and Betty Hicks, James Hicks, Arnold and Gloria Himelstein, Goldie and George Hirsberg, Paula Jackson, Michael James, Wesley "Junebug" Jefferson, Patricia Johnson, Aaron Kline, Wanda Lee, Jon Levingston, Bill Luckett, Lawrence Magdovitz, Dorothy Antici Middleton, Joe Middleton, Sarah Moore, Jacqueline Nassar, Joyce Ordway, Red Paden, Lin "Pap" Pang, Bill "Howlin' Mad" Perry, Shelley Ritter, Lou Ruskey, Emma Ruskey, Alcorn Russell, Anthony Sherrod, Josh Stewart, Roger Stolle, the Sunflower River Blues Association, Attilio Tarzi, Bobby Tarzi, Jimmy Tarzi, C.V. Veal, Lee Williams, Venessia Young.